FRENCH POLITICS
IN TRANSITION:
The Years After DeGaulle

Roy C. Macridis

Brandeis University

Winthrop Publishers, Inc.
Cambridge, Massachusetts

Library of Congress Cataloging in Publication Data

Macridis, Roy C
  French politics in transition.

  Bibliography: p.
  1. France—Politics and government—1958-
I. Title.
JN2594.2.M3   320.9'44'083   74-28425
ISBN 0-87626-309-0
ISBN 0-87626-308-2 pbk.

... In contrast with the individualistic way of life as country-dwellers, craftsmen, tradesmen and rentiers, which had been that of their forefathers for centuries Frenchmen now found themselves, not without some distress, forced into a mechanized mass existence. Work, in factories, workshops, mills, dockyards, stores, demanded uniformly mechanical and repetitive movements in well-established grooves and with always the same companies. . . . Everyone now lived in a kind of cell or nondescript block. Grey, faceless crowds travelled in public transport, and one could neither drive nor walk along a street without being herded into lanes and regimented by signs. Even leisure had become collective and prescribed. . . . All this was due to force of circumstances, but I knew it weighed more heavily on our people, by reason of their nature and antecedents, than on any other, and felt that some sudden provocation might well precipitate them one day into some irrational crisis.

General Charles DeGaulle
Memoirs of Hope: Renewal and Endeavor

Contents

Preface

For a long time a number of students of French politics, including myself, assumed that the Gaullist regime, providing for reinforced executive leadership and stability, was a temporary one and that upon DeGaulle's demise France would revert to a multiparty political society with unstable and shifting coalition cabinets and weakened executive leadership. DeGaulle resigned from the presidency in April, 1969, and died in November of 1970 at the age of eighty. Thus we have had at least five years to test the viability of the Gaullist institutions.

They seem to have survived the test. What accounts for this? It is in part the purpose of this book to try to answer this question. The book also discusses the prospects of renewed crises that may incite the French once more to question the legitimacy of their present political institutions. One such crisis occurred in May–June, 1969. Workers, students and virtually most citizens from all walks of life rose against the omnipotent and impersonal State, bringing the economy to a standstill and almost tearing apart the fabric of the society. The intensity and scale of the "revolution" was unprecedented. Never at least since the Paris Commune of 1871 had anything like it happened. Social and economic pent-up demands may again account for a recurrence. The demand for the "reform of the society" is just as pervasive today as the reform of the political institutions was ever since the Liberation of France. The years to come will be either years of social and administrative reform or of very profound social turbulence.

Will the institutions and the new President be able to provide an answer? It is my conclusion that they can. For side by side with institutional reforms there have been profound social changes that have injected an element of pragmatism and even conservatism in the political attitudes and behavior of the average French citizen. The need for reform is often the child of affluence and prosperity but the latter inhibit violence and revolution. The political parties are in the process of becoming meaningful vehicles for reform and change rather than remain advocates of sectarian and ideological positions calling the citizen to direct action. The workers themselves are not likely to throw away the gains that they either wrenched from the reluctant *patrons* or had bestowed upon them by DeGaulle's paternal regime. Everything points to stability, peaceful change and reform, the structuring and the organization of the citizen into national party coalitions and hence to a genuine dialogue between "government" and "opposition." France may be entering, at a time when most Western democracies, including Great Britain and the United States, have experienced severe political crises that have thwarted political action and decision-making, a period of stability and consensus. We cannot yet say it is definitive. It corresponds to a transitional phase that points to the full legitimization of its institutions and to an orderly deliberation and resolution of issues and conflicts. It is still a fragile situation. It is also at the mercy of outside and adventitious forces—a worldwide depression; a collapse of whatever is left of the world monetary system; adverse developments within the other Common Market countries, to say nothing of a return to a period of international tensions and conflicts.

To my best knowledge this is the only study available to the American students and public that attempts to deal in some detail with French politics as they have developed since DeGaulle's death. Whatever my own opinions might be, the material presented will help the students, I hope, to draw their own conclusions.

I wish to thank my wife, Jacklyn, and my daughter, Kathy, for the help they gave me in the last stages of this manuscript. Mrs. Barbara Nagy typed the first draft. I am also grateful to the Guggenheim Foundation for a grant to spend a year in Paris and also for their help in making it possible for me to visit France during the legislative election of March 1973. My thanks also to Dr. Marver Bernstein, President of Brandeis University, for a small grant enabling me to visit France during the presidential election of May 1974. My old friend, James Murray, III, now President of Winthrop Publishers, was, as always, a source of encouragement.

Terms and Abbreviations

PSU–*Parti Socialiste Unifié* (Unified Socialist Party): Despite the name, it is a splinter group consisting of members of the Socialist party and others who refused to support DeGaulle when he returned to politics to prepare the new Constitution and become President of the Fifth Republic in 1958. Its membership is around 15,000.

Parti Socialiste (Socialist Party): The renovated old S.F.I.O. (*Section Française de l'Internationale Ouvrière*) established in 1969. In 1971 members of various political clubs and splinter formations entered into the Party and François Mitterrand became its leader.

CDP–*Centre Démocratie et Progrès* (Center for Democracy and Progress): The centrist group that supported Pompidou in the election of 1969 and became a part of the "presidential majority." In 1973 it ran in the legislative election as a part of the Gaullist majority. In the 1974 presidential election it supported the Gaullist candidate Chaban-Delmas on the first ballot but then switched to support Giscard d'Estaing on the second ballot.

PDM–*Progrès et Démocratie Moderne:* Larger centrist formation opposed to the Gaullist government until 1969. The CDP emerged from the PDM.

Centre Démocrate: Centrist group under Lecanuet, founded after the presidential election of 1965 in which Lecanuet received about 15 percent of the votes on the first ballot. Consisted mostly of leaders of the MRP (*Mouvement Républicain Populaire*) and some other centrists.

Radical Socialist Party: The grand old party of the Third Republic with strong left-wing program but centrist votes. It declined rapidly during the Fifth Republic and by 1965 it did not have more than 20,000 members. Some of its leaders moved to the center and others maintained their connection with the Left. In 1969 Jean-Jacques Servan-Schreiber became its leader. Its new title is *Parti Radical* (Radical Party).

Réformateurs: Political group formed in 1972 that included the Radical Socialists under Jean-Jacques Servan-Schreiber and the Democratic Center under Jean Lecanuet. It opposed the Gaullists, but in 1974 it supported Giscard d'Estaing and became a member of the new presidential majority.

"Left-wing Radicals": Members and leaders of the old Radical Socialist party who refused to enter into the *Réformateur* group and remained allied with the Socialists and the Communists both in the election of 1973 and the presidential election of 1974. It is a splinter group with not more than 600,000 votes.

RI–*Républicains Indépendants* (Independent Republicans): Group of independents who after 1962 supported DeGaulle and formed a part of the

Gaullist and Pompidou majority. In 1967, 1968, and 1973 they ran in the legislative elections together with the Gaullists. Their leader, Giscard d'Estaing, was elected President of the Republic in 1974. A small party with not more than 25,000 members and not more than 7 percent of the national vote.

"The Majority": The term majority, used throughout the book, applies to the pro-Gaullist coalition consisting of the UDR, the RI, and the CPD. It stood behind DeGaulle and Pompidou and is now giving its support to the government of Giscard d'Estaing. The *Réformateurs* have been added to it since 1974.

URP–*Union des Démocrates Pour la République* or *Union pour la Défense de la République* (Union of the Democrats for the Republic or Union for the Defense of the Republic): The Gaullist formation. The term "Gaullists" is synonomous with it. It is the last party label given to the Gaullists. In the 1950's the Gaullist party was the RPF–*Rassemblement du Peuple Français* (Rally of the French People). In 1958 it was called UNR: *Union pour la Nouvelle République* (Union for the New Republic); in 1967 it was the UNR-UDT—the latter three letters standing for *Union Démocratique du Travail*—(Democratic Union of Labor) to indicate the social and reformist wing of the Party. In 1968 it was the UD–Ve standing for *Union Démocratique–Ve* (Democratic Union–Fifth Republic).

PCF–*Parti Communist Français* (Communist Party of France).

CFDT–*Confédération Française Démocratique du Travail* (French Democratic Confederation of Labor): Trade Union with about 700,000 members. Emerged from the CFTC (the Christian Confederation of Labor) in 1964, by abandoning its religious identity.

CGT–*Confédération Generale du Travail:* Trade Union with about 1,600,000 members. Closely affiliated with the Communist party.

F.O.–*Force Ouvrière:* Labor Force. Trade Union with not more than 400,000 members. Refused to remain within the CGT under Communist influence, to remain close to the Socialist party.

FEN–*Fédération de l'Éducation Nationale* (Federation of National Education): Large umbrella federation including most of the teachers and professors. The membership of the unions that are affiliated with it is estimated at about 500,000.

To Jacklyn . . .

chapter one

The Gaullist Legacy

To many students the name DeGaulle and his period spanning almost thirty years between 1940 to 1970 is remote history. "Gaullism" is becoming an historical landmark like the New Deal, World War II and Nazi Germany. The very title of this chapter, "The Gaullist Legacy," is an admission that we are dealing with such a landmark. Gaullism represents a mixture of practices, policies, and institutional reforms, as well as economic and social changes. Both powerful historical forces and needs and outside pressures account for it. Gaullism has shaped the post–World War II history of France, left an indelible imprint upon its present politics and institutions, and accounts for a political movement in whose name contemporary political leaders—young and old—continue to speak.

The "Gaullist System"

The term "system" here refers to a set of institutions; perhaps more important, it also refers to a set of values and beliefs shared in common by the people which became accepted only when they were clearly formulated and institutionalized by DeGaulle and his associates. In a sense DeGaulle obeyed powerful, if latent, national imperatives. No matter how implausible it may sound, his system would have had to be invented or somebody playing a similar role would have had to appear. In old nations the parameters of freedom and discretion within which political leaders can move are narrow; success or failure is often determined by the leaders' ability to express and to formulate policies and reforms in line with basic national demands. DeGaulle did this—with persistence, clarity and conviction.

Throughout French political history, two major forces have been at work, never quite reaching—at least not yet—a compromise. One force is the quest for national and political unity through a system that submerges individual and group particularisms and unites the disparate contending political families. Monarchy and Bonapartism are two political forms that express it. But the second force, equally powerful and

2

persistent, is the pervasiveness of different and conflicting political ideologies, social classes and interests, and manifold particularisms. It found its best expression in "Republicanism" as it developed in France after 1871 with full legislative supremacy, and a weak Executive. The "republican synthesis," as it has often been called, allowed particularisms to flourish. But it also provided, under certain conditions, for a certain stability based upon a precarious and temporary compromise among the various ideological and political conflicts.

Ever since the French Revolution, there has been a constant dialectic between the quest for unity and the assertion of particularisms— between the Republican tradition on the one hand and the Monarchical or Bonapartist on the other. The quest for unity—but not necessarily its successful implementation—emerges whenever there is an international crisis in which the security of the nation is in jeopardy; whenever there are serious foreign policy crises that divide the nation; and whenever such divisions aggravate existing domestic conflicts and sharpen the struggle among competing political forces. All that is needed, then, for the quest for unity to assert itself is a leader who can play the role of political and national unifier. In contrast, particularisms dominate in times of general domestic prosperity and international tranquility.

DeGaulle's system represents a genuine effort to reconcile these two powerful traditions—particularisms with unity, individual and group interests with state authority. In other words, to bring together elements of the unifying (Monarchical or Bonapartist) tradition and the particularist (Republican) one. The basic pillars on which his system was built were: 1. a strong nation-state, with a strong and independent Executive; 2. a representative assembly with limited powers to express particularisms and adjudicate conflicts of interest; and 3. a participating citizenry so that the head of the state would be in close contact with the people, and would consult them in major national policy options. Relatedly every effort was to be made to eradicate the basic reasons for internal conflicts, especially through economic modernization and social reforms, ultimately reducing the distance between social classes, and to provide for rapid social mobility, mainly through education, and for rapid economic growth.

A STRONG NATION-STATE

To understand DeGaulle as a political figure we must understand his unswerving attachment to his country. France in his eyes was more than its territory and its people and its history. It was a superior way of life, the flowering of the Western values of freedom, tolerance, humanism. This is the opening paragraph of his *Memoirs:*

All my life I have thought of France in a certain way. This is inspired by sentiment as much as by reason. . . . France is not really herself unless in the front rank; that only vast enterprises are capable of counterbalancing the ferments of dispersal which are inherent in her people. . . . France cannot be France without greatness.[1]

He concludes the same volume in the following terms:

Pouring over the gulf into which the country has fallen, I am her son, calling her, holding the light for her, showing her the way of rescue. Many people have joined me already. Others will come, I am sure. I can hear France now, answering me. In the depths of the abyss she is rising up again, she is on the march, she is climbing the slope. Ah! Mother, such as we are, we are here to serve you.[2]

His life coincided with a period when French national power declined. He made an heroic effort to revive it. The defeat of the French army by the Nazis, the subsequent emergence of American power to which the European nations, including France, became subordinated, the inevitable disintegration of the French Empire in the face of new-born nationalisms around the world, and finally the war of independence in Algeria —all were indicative of France's weakness. Similarly, the inability of the political system at home to utilize fully its technology and science for the purpose of modernization were also a sign of decline. DeGaulle's answer—in line with the realities of the situation—was 1. to try to arrest and reverse the decline in French power; 2. to reestablish the authority of the State; and 3. to proceed rapidly with economic modernization.

The French, demoralized by decades of internal conflict and defeats, found in this national assertiveness a fulfillment of their own pent-up demands and desires. DeGaulle's independent stance received wide approbation; his nuclear independent posture became progressively accepted. A reborn nationalism swept the country. His popularity remained remarkably high—despite sporadic downswings—when he was head of the Provisional Government (1944–1946) and throughout his presidency (1958–1969).

THE STATE

If the nation is a reality, how does it manifest itself? The vehicle of national expression is the State. DeGaulle was heir to the French revolutionary tradition of a strong, centralized, republican state, but also to the tradition of a strong, central administration under the French monarchy. The State is supreme; it represents the collective interest, and must implement values and provide for social and economic services. It is the embodiment of the collective will of the nation. Where it ceases to exist, there is chaos and conflict; where it is strong and active, there is order and justice and freedom. DeGaulle was a "statist" in the sense that he believed that side by side with the individual, parties, groups, organizations, and interests, the State had an ultimate and comprehensive role to play.

A devout Catholic and a military man, DeGaulle had never done or said anything to deride the Republic in France. Upon the liberation of France in 1944 he proceeded to rebuild the Republic and ultimately to allow it to go its own way. Again in 1958—when he returned to office as President of the Republic—he reaffirmed his faith in the republican institutions and became the architect of a constitution that preserves the heart of a republican state, with free elections, free popular consultations, free parties, free speech, and freedom of assembly. However, this does not necessarily mean that DeGaulle was a republican by preference or conviction. The Republic appeared to him to be the only viable political form for France. A statesman, like a weaver, must work with the material he has. A greater number of Frenchmen can live together under the Republic than under any other system. History and tradition have woven the fabric—to tear it apart was to endanger the nation. The fabric must be rewoven stronger than ever. The Fifth Republic, established at a time when France seemed to be on the brink of civil war, is what in DeGaulle's mind best reconciled leadership with political participation; representation of interests and government for national interest; freedom and stability; popular control with central direction.

A major defect of the Third (1871–1940) and especially of the Fourth (1946–1958) Republics, according to DeGaulle, was the concentration of all powers in the hands of a divided representative assembly, thus undermining the authority of the State. It established a weak presidency with no authority to speak for France concerning major internal problems and, more particularly, foreign policy and defense, and a weak cabinet with no independent executive power. The State became so weakened that it could not represent the nation, since the system itself put the premium on particularisms—local, party, and interest—from which no national purpose could emerge. DeGaulle's thoughts here probed one of the most critical and unresolved problems of politics—that of the national will. His resolution of the problem was to view political life at two levels. One is the level at which particular and group interests constantly act and interact. They must be given a large degree of latitude since their activity is essential for the release of the mainsprings of individual interest and action. But while DeGaulle maintained that such freedom is essential, he argued that it is not adequate. A system must also provide its citizens with the possibility to contemplate issues that go beyond their specific professions, interests, or roles. A citizen is more than the sum total of the interests he represents or the roles he performs. This is the second level of discourse; according to DeGaulle, the Third and Fourth Republics were at fault for not having instituted mechanisms to provide for leadership and representation on the broader issues that transcended particular ones. While interests thrived, purpose was at a standstill; while particularisms flourished, the whole slumbered; while each one was represented in parliament, the voice of the nation was not heard; while the "individual" was solicited in elections, the "citizen" was ignored. As a result, the political community was reduced to warring and irreconcilable factions and the nation-state was allowed to disintegrate.[3]

THE CONSTITUTION OF THE FIFTH REPUBLIC

In an effort to bring unity and at the same time give the particularisms their free expression, DeGaulle proposed a Constitution (overwhelmingly accepted in 1958) that brought together elements of Bonapartism and Republicanism. The Constitution established a strong Executive in the form of a President with independent powers to govern and a cabinet headed by a Prime Minister responsible to a popularly elected assembly. The underlying theory (especially when it was decided to elect the President by direct universal suffrage in 1962) was that the President would embody and represent the major national interests of the country—particularly its foreign policy and defense—and act in time of national crisis. He was to be the ultimate guarantor of the functioning of the institutions and the preservation of national integrity. Particularisms, on the other hand, were given free expression in the legislature, freely elected by the people organized through political parties and interest associations. This was not a concession to the republican tradition but an expression of a genuine belief that "parliament" had an important role to play and that it should be given every opportunity to play it. In this sense the Gaullist system was a synthesis of the Bonapartist or Monarchical tradition and the Republican one, bringing together the two levels of governing—the "high level" of national will, expressed through the presidency, and the "low level" of particularisms expressed through the legislature. Or, as Williams and Harrison write, a reconciliation between "noble politics" and "common politics."[4]

The Legal Framework[5]

The landscape of the new constitution seemed familiar at first. The executive power is shared by the President of the Republic and the Prime Minister with his cabinet. The legislative power is vested in the National Assembly and Senate. The government (the Prime Minister and the cabinet) is responsible before Parliament.

The Executive: The President of the Republic. The President was to be the "keystone of the arch" of the new Republic—both the symbol and the instrument of reinforced Executive authority. Elected after the constitutional reform of 1962 directly by the people, he is given personal powers that he can exercise solely at his discretion. The President designates the Prime Minister. Though it is presumed that such a designation will be made with an eye to the existing party configuration in the National Assembly, it is a personal discretionary act. He can dissolve the National Assembly at any time, on any issue, and for any reason. There is only one limitation—he cannot dissolve twice within the same year; and one formality—he must "consult" with the Prime Minister and the presidents of the two legislative assemblies.

When the institutions of the Republic, the independence of the nation, the integrity of its territory, or the execution of international engagements are menaced in a grave and immediate manner and the regular functioning of the public powers is interrupted, the President may take measures necessitated by the circumstances (Article 16). Again this is a personal and discretionary act. The President is required only to inform the nation by a message and to "consult" the Constitutional Council. The National Assembly, however, reconvenes automatically and cannot be dissolved during the emergency period.

The Constitution also explicitly vests in the President other powers that he can exercise at his discretion. He has the nominating power for all civil and military posts and, unless it is otherwise provided by an organic law, he signs all decrees and ordinances prepared by the Council of Ministers. He can raise the question of unconstitutionality on a bill or on a law before the Constitutional Council. He presides over the meetings of the Council of Ministers, receives ambassadors, and sends messages to Parliament. He may ask for the reexamination of a bill or some of its articles, which cannot be refused; he negotiates and ratifies treaties, and is kept informed of all negotiations leading to the conclusion of international agreements; he is commander-in-chief and presides over the Committee of National Defense.

Finally, the President can bring certain issues before the people in a referendum:

> The President of the Republic on the proposal of the government . . . or on joint resolution by the two legislative assemblies . . . *may* submit to a referendum any bill dealing with the organization of the public powers, the approval of an agreement of the Community or the authorization to ratify a treaty, that without being contrary to the Constitution would affect the functioning of existing institutions (Article 11).

Calling a referendum is, however, a personal act of the President of the Republic. He may elicit or refuse it depending on the circumstances.

The Constitution explicitly consecrates the large influence of the President over the functioning of the institutions and policy-making:

> The President of the Republic shall see that the Constitution is respected. He shall ensure, by his arbitration, the regular functioning of the governmental authorities, as well as the continuance of the State.
>
> He shall be the guarantor of national independence, of the integrity of the territory, and of respect for . . . agreements and treaties (Article 5).

Mediation is a personal act involving the exercise of judgment. As a result, the President is given implicitly a veto power on almost every conceivable aspect of policy. He may refuse to sign a decree or to make a nomination. He may dissolve or threaten to dissolve the National Assembly and call for a referendum. He becomes an integral part of policy-making and policy execution despite the fact that he is not responsible to the legislature.

The list of presidential prerogatives is thus an impressive one. The framers, while rejecting presidential government, wished nonetheless to establish a president who could act on his own. In matters of war, foreign policy, the preservation of internal peace, and the functioning of the institutions, his powers are overriding and he can bring them to bear upon every type of policy and decision. His acts have a political content.

The Government.　The government, composed of the Prime Minister and his ministers, "determines and conducts the policy of the nation" and is "responsible before the Parliament." Special recognition is accorded to the Prime Minister. He "directs" the action of the government and is "responsible" for the national defense. He "assures the execution of the laws and exercises the rule-making power" (Articles 20 and 21). He determines the composition of his cabinet, presides over its meetings, and directs the administrative services. He defends his policy before the Parliament, answers questions addressed to him by the members of parliament, states the overall program of the government in special programmatic declarations, and in general "governs" while it enjoys the confidence of a majority in the National Assembly.

The Legislature.　The Parliament of the Fifth Republic is, as in the past, bicameral. It consists of a National Assembly and a Senate. The National Assembly, elected for five years by universal suffrage, is composed of 490 deputies (483 from metropolitan France, and 17 from overseas Departments and territories). The Senate, elected for nine years, is composed of 260 members. It is elected indirectly by the municipal councilors, the departmental councilors, and the members of the National Assembly. One-third of its membership is renewed every three years. The two chambers have equal powers except in two respects: the traditional prerogative of the lower chamber to examine the budget first is maintained, and the Senate cannot introduce a motion of censure and initiate the fall of the cabinet.

Article 45 specifies that every bill "is examined successively in the two assemblies with a view to the adoption of an identical text." But if there is continuing disagreement on the text of a bill after two readings by each assembly, the Prime Minister can convene a "joint conference committee," consisting of an equal number of members of the two chambers, to propose a compromise text. This text may be submitted by the government for the approval of the two assemblies. It is only in case of a persistent discord between the two assemblies that the Prime Minister *may* ask the National Assembly to rule "definitively." Thus, the National Assembly has the last word and the Senate a veto power, depending upon the attitude of the government. If the government and the Senate are in accord, the senatorial veto is ironclad. The Senate can be overruled only if there is an agreement between the government and the National Assembly.

A Rationalized Parliament. The Constitution establishes a "rationalized Parliament" in a number of ways. Only two sessions of the two assemblies are allowed, for a total of five and one-half months. Extraordinary sessions may take place at the request of the Prime Minister or of a majority of the members of the National Assembly "on a specific agenda." The sessions are convened and closed by a decree of the President of the Republic. The law-making functions of the Parliament are restricted to matters defined in the Constitution. The government can legislate on all other matters by simple decree. The legislative agenda is no longer the outcome of interminable debates between the president of the National Assembly, the presidents of the parliamentary groups, and a government delegate. The government now fixes the order of business. The president of the National Assembly is elected for the whole legislative term, thus avoiding annual elections that in the past placed him at the mercy of the various parliamentary groups. The Senate elects its president every three years.

The Parliament can no longer establish its own standing orders. They must be approved by the Constitutional Council before they become effective. The number of parliamentary committees is reduced and their functions carefully circumscribed. Only six committees are allowed by the Constitution. It is further stated that the government text of a bill and not the committees' amendments and counterproposals, as under the Fourth Republic, come before the floor. The government has the right to reject all amendments and to demand a vote on its own text. This procedure is known as the "blocked vote."

Relations Between Parliament and Government. Four major provisions determine the nature of the relations between Parliament and the government: (1) the incompatibility between the parliamentary mandate and a cabinet post; (2) the manner in which the responsibility of the cabinet before the Parliament comes into play; (3) the distinction between "legislation" and "rule-making"; and (4) the introduction of the "executive budget."

1. *The Rule of Incompatibility.* Article 23 of the Constitution is explicit: "The 'office' of members of government is incompatible with the exercise of any parliamentary mandate." Thus, a member of Parliament who joins the cabinet must resign his mandate for the balance of the legislative term. He is replaced in Parliament by the person whose name appeared together with his on the ballot—the *suppléant* (substitute). Nonparliamentarians may become cabinet members. Despite the rule of incompatibility, cabinet members sit in Parliament and participate freely in the debates.

2. *Responsibility of the Cabinet Before the Legislature.* The responsibility of the cabinet to the legislature comes into play in a number of ways. After the Prime Minister has been nominated by the President of the Republic, he presents his program before the National Assembly. This statement calls for a vote in favor or against. In the first case, the cabinet is "invested," while in the second case, the Prime Minister must submit his resignation to the President of the Republic. A vote by simple majority against the Prime Minister and his program is all that is required to dismiss the designated government at this stage.

    After the cabinet has been invested, its responsibility to Parliament can be engaged in the following manner: the National Assembly has the right to introduce a motion of censure, which must be signed by one-tenth of the members of the National Assembly. The vote on the motion takes place forty-eight hours after it has been introduced. The motion is lost unless it receives an absolute majority in the National Assembly. Blank ballots and abstentions count for the government. If the motion is carried, the government must resign; if the motion is lost, then its signatories cannot move another one in the course of the same legislative session.

    The Prime Minister may, after consultation with the cabinet, stake the life of his government on any general issue of policy or on any given legislative text. Although the Constitution does not use the term, this is equivalent to putting the "question of confidence." In the first case, declaring a general policy is presumed to be accepted unless there is a motion of censure voted under the conditions mentioned previously. In the second case, the bill becomes law unless a motion of censure is introduced and voted according to the same conditions, but with one difference: the same signatories may introduce a motion of censure as many times as the Prime Minister stakes his government's responsibility. Thus, if the motion is carried by an absolute majority, the bill does not become law and the government resigns. If, however, the motion is lost, even if carried by a relative majority, then the text becomes law and the government stays in office.

3. *"Law" and "Rule-making."* The Constitution provides, in accordance with the canons of parliamentary government, that "law is voted by Parliament." Members of Parliament and of the government can introduce bills and amendments. The scope of law-making, however, is defined in the Constitution (Article 34) to include:

> . . . the *regulations* concerning:
> civil rights and the fundamental guarantees granted to the citizens for the exercise of their public liberties; . . .
> nationality, status and legal capacity of persons, marriage contracts, inheritance and gifts;
> determination of crimes and misdemeanors as well as the penalties imposed therefor; criminal procedure; . . .
> the basis, the rate and the methods of collecting taxes of all types; the issuance of currency; . . .
> the electoral system of the Parliamentary assemblies and the local assemblies; . . .
> the nationalization of enterprises and the transfer of the property of enterprises from the public to the private sector; . . .
> [and the] fundamental *principles* of:
> the general organization of national defense;
> the free administration of local communities, the extent of their jurisdiction and their resources;
> education;
> property rights, civil and commercial obligations;
> legislation pertaining to employment, unions and social security.

This enumeration of legislative power is limited. Article 37 makes this point clear. "All other matters," it states, "than those which are in the domain of law fall within the rule-making sphere." The same article and other provisions of the Constitution ensure the distinction between legislation and rule-making for the future by a series of safety devices. If a bill is debated before the Parliament and the government contests the Assembly's competence, then the bill is referred to the Constitutional Council. If a bill is enacted by Parliament but there are doubts about the Parliament's jurisdiction, then the President of the Republic, the Prime Minister, or one of the presidents of the two assemblies can bring it before the Constitutional Council before it is promulgated. If a bill is passed and promulgated, even then it can be brought before the Constitutional Council on the ground that it deals with a matter that was beyond

Parliament's competence. Finally, the government in the future can modify by simple decree a law passed by the legislature, provided the Constitutional Council decides that the Parliament exceeded its competence in passing it.

4. *The Budget.* The Constitution introduces the "executive budget." The budget is submitted by the government to Parliament. Proposals stemming from members of Parliament "are not receivable if their adoption entails either a diminution of public resources or an increase in public expenditures (Article 47)." No bill entailing diminution of resources or additional expenditures is receivable at any time.

These then are the great lines of the constitutional structure: bicameralism giving the Senate a genuine veto even over budgetary policy if it has the support of the government; a division between law-making and rule-making that in effect gives to the Executive broad legislative powers; the possibility that bills become law unless there is an absolute majority against the cabinet rather than a majority for the bill; delegation of law-making power to the Executive; priority to the government bills introduced in Parliament; the ever-present threat of dissolution; numerous devices in the hands of the President of the Republic and the Prime Minister to suspend legislation by appealing to the Constitutional Council and, finally, the possibility of a referendum to override the legislature.

The Constitutional Council. The most striking innovation made by the framers of the new Constitution was the Constitutional Council, composed of nine members who serve for a period of nine years. Three are nominated by the President of the Republic, three by the president of the National Assembly, and three by the president of the Senate. The Council is renewed by a third every three years. In addition, all former Presidents of the Republic are members *ex officio.*

A variety of powers have been given to the Constitutional Council. It supervises the presidential elections and the referendums and proclaims the results; it judges the validity of all contested legislative elections, thus avoiding bitter and long controversies in the legislative assemblies. It is the ultimate court of appeal in interpreting the Constitution on a limited number of matters. Thus, all bills, including treaties, may be referred to it before their promulgation by the President of the Republic, the Prime Minister, or one of the presidents of the two assemblies. A declaration of unconstitutionality suspends the promulgation of the bill or the application of the treaty. It judges the constitutionality of all standing orders and organic laws, which go before it automatically. It is, finally, the guardian of legislative–executive relations in all matters concerning the respective legislative competence of the two branches.

The constitutional review provided by the Constitution of the Fifth Republic differs from the American practice in two important respects. First, it is limited to certain specified categories of cases involving the relationship of governmental organs; and second, it is brought into play only upon the request of four officers of the Fifth Republic— the President, the Prime Minister, and the two presidents of the legislative assemblies. Review applies only to impending bills. A law cannot be attacked for "unconstitutionality" except under the specific and very restrictive terms of Article 37—that is, only when the government claims that the legislature exceeded its competence in enacting it. In contrast to the American practice, the Constitutional Council is the guardian of the constitutional provisions regarding executive–legislative relations with particular reference to law-making rather than the ultimate court of appeal for the protection of the law of the land at the request of an individual against legislative or administrative infringements.

Concerning the amending process, the Constitution provides that initiative belongs to the President of the Republic on the proposal of the Prime Minister and to the members of Parliament. An amendment proposed by the two legislative assemblies by simple majorities becomes effective only after it is approved in a referendum. A proposal stemming from the President and approved by a three-fifths majority of the two chambers, meeting jointly in a congress, comes into effect without a referendum unless the President decides to call for one.

The Evolution of the Constitution

It was through this constitutional structure—in which the scale was heavily tipped in favor of the Executive branch—that DeGaulle expected to reestablish the authority of the State while giving free expression to the political forces in the country. In the last analysis, the President held a powerful veto through his power of dissolution— which he used in 1962 when a motion of censure was passed against his Prime Minister, and in 1968 though no such censure motion had been passed. He also held the ultimate weapon of special emergency powers in case of grave disorders, a power that he used once during the Algerian war and that he was tempted to use again in 1968. Elected for a period of seven years and subject to no other censure than a trial for high treason by a special tribunal, the French President enjoyed powers that most American Presidents would envy!

The Constitution evolved throughout the Gaullist period—and, as we shall see, during Pompidou's presidency—in the direction of presidential dominance. The President claimed to represent the national sovereignty and stated that all offices and authorities derived from him. He not only appointed but dismissed his Prime Minister at will; he also appointed and dismissed cabinet members with only the formal assent of his Prime Minister; he decided on policy issues without consulting his Prime Minister and cabinet; he created an "office of the Presidency" staffed with experts that elaborated and made policy and through which he directed the activities of the Ministries; he met with his cabinet—not to reach collective decisions but to hear views before deciding himself; he used the referendum to revise the Constitution without consulting, as required, the legislature; he allowed his Prime Minister to assume office and govern without first seeking the endorsement of the National Assembly; he intervened actively in the elections of 1962, 1967 and 1968 by asking the people to vote for his supporters—the "majority"—thus assuming a direct political role; he was solely responsible for negotiations with the Algerian rebels and the ultimate recognition of Algerian independence, which was granted in July 1962; he directed foreign policy, without any consultations with his Prime Minister and the cabinet, through his Foreign Minister who faithfully implemented his instructions; he assumed the sole power to convene or refuse to convene extraordinary sessions of the legislature despite the letter of the Constitution to the contrary. Presidential dominance became the reality of French political life.[6]

This evolution, however, was made possible because of reasons that neither the framers of the Constitution nor DeGaulle himself anticipated. For DeGaulle's overwhelming powers and popularity produced in the legislature (the National Assembly) a majority. Whatever its various party labels the Gaullist movement assumed, it consisted of members that pledged fidelity to the President—DeGaulle. DeGaulle stood above the Gaullist movement; he never accepted to become its leader; it was a mass of followers. This movement in the name of DeGaulle, and by pledging its fidelity to DeGaulle, gained a majority, sometimes alone and sometimes in cooperation with satellite parties. It has held a majority since 1962. This "majority" made presidential government possible. There were no conflicts between the National Assembly and the government on the one hand and the President on the other. Both the majority and the government owed their position to the President. To resist him or for the National Assembly to resist his designated Prime Minister and cabinet would mean a confrontation with the President, to whom they had pledged their support.

Since the inception of the Fifth Republic only one motion of censure succeeded by the requisite absolute majority—in 1962. Some twenty other motions of censure were introduced between 1958 to 1974. They all failed. As long as the majority holds and as long as the majority hails from the President, he can count on it to support his (and his government's) policies. This is the key to presidential dominance: it is the real "keystone of the arch" of presidential government, by far more important than the constitutionally derived powers of the President.

There are two anomalies in the Gaullist Constitution as it has evolved in the direction of presidential dominance. One is the manner in which referendums were held; the second lies in the organization of the Executive. Both may in the future cause serious problems for the President. Under DeGaulle the referendum became synonomous with a plebiscite. Whatever the policy issue involved—the adoption of the Constitution (1958), "self-determination for Algeria" (1961); Algerian independence (1962); the revision of the Constitution to provide for the direct popular election of the President (1962); the reform of the Senate and the establishment of regional government (1969)—it was also a vote of confidence in DeGaulle. The President asked every time for a massive approbation of *his* policy, threatening to resign if he did not receive adequate support. Thus the referendum became transformed, in the best Bonapartist tradition, into a plebiscite. The personal element overshadowed the policy issue before the people. On four occasions DeGaulle won. But in the last referendum of 1969 there was no massive vote for him and his reforms. In fact he lost—and had to resign.

The second anomaly is far more serious. It is embedded in the Constitution itself, and cannot be evaded. A President may decide not to resort to a referendum or, even better, not to transform it into a vote for or against him. But under certain conditions he cannot evade a potential conflict with a Prime Minister. For while the Constitution gives individual and personal powers to the President, it also establishes a parliamentary system giving power directly to the Prime Minister who is responsible before the National Assembly. It includes, in other words, a powerful parliamentary component. In fact, many commentators have argued that there are two constitutions and not one. The first consecrates presidential government; the second makes parliamentary government possible. As long as there is a majority in the National Assembly for the President, the Prime Minister is the President's man. Presidential leadership will continue. But if there is a majority in Parliament *against* the designated Prime Minister and hence against the President, a Prime Minister designated by the President will be censured by such a hostile majority. The President may dissolve and call for an election, thus directly engaging his own political responsibility by supporting his designated Prime Minister. If the same hostile majority is re-elected, a conflict between its leader and the President—between the National Assembly and the President—cannot be evaded. At this point the legislature may resume its powers forcing the President either to resign or to give in to the majority and appoint *its* leader as Prime Minister. In either case presidential dominance will be seriously threatened, if not destroyed. The parliamentary component of the constitution will gain ascendance; presidential dominance will wither away.

Participation

The strengthening of the Executive at the expense of the legislature produced a series of phenomena, all part of the Gaullist system. First, a great number of ministerial posts were given to technicians. These men never held an electoral office but came from the administrative services that recruited from the elite schools of France—notably the École Nationale d'Administration, established in 1946. It is true that as the system evolved the number of parliamentarians assuming cabinet posts increased—but this is deceptive. Many ran for office *after* they had secured ministerial recognition and prominence. They were above all technicians and managers, concerned with doing things, providing for services, establishing plans for economic development, running the public social and economic services. They were the "technocrats"—with an eye to efficiency and pragmatic choices, to statistics and economic charts. They were servants of the State rather than elected representatives of the people.

There was a corresponding trend on the part of the interest groups to reach out and influence the administrative agencies and the ministers rather than Parliament. A growing osmosis between interest groups and the administration developed but it was primarily the big financial and industrial interests that were heard. The workers remained divided into many unions and some have resisted until recently the dialogue because of ideological reasons. But they as well as the farmers' associations began to follow the same pattern and seek out negotiations and arrangements with administrators.

While lip service was paid to decentralization, DeGaulle and his cabinet together with the administrative services exemplified the overriding competence of a highly centralized state. Paris would decide where to build schools; where to create a new refinery and steel complex; where and how to channel investments to one region rather than another; how to allocate subsidies. The more the Gaullists talked of participation the more the State appeared remote from the average citizen, from the municipalities and the towns and the various planning regional councils and even from the political parties. It was ironic that DeGaulle's last year as President was devoted to repeated exhortations to develop participatory mechanisms in education, in planning, in regional development and to provide for some system of regional autonomy.

Are we then to say that the second pillar of the Gaullist edifice—participation—had failed? Yes and no. Participation can be viewed at many levels. First, the election of the President by direct popular suffrage produced a drastic change in the electoral habits of the French; it ultimately influenced the political parties. A presidential election gave to the electorate an opportunity to choose directly a man with a program to govern or at least to provide the basic orientations for governing. This provides a direct link between the citizenry and the government that had not existed before. Under a multiparty system the French had to submit to coalition cabinets formed by parties and leaders, none of whom had been given a direct mandate to govern. The presidential election was precisely such a mandate. Second, referendums provided for periodic consultations, in which the people could approve or disapprove directly certain contemplated policies. Third, the political parties under the impact of presidential government began to change their ways. They began to coalesce into large coalitions and to present a "program of government" providing in fact a choice between two contesting points of view. Many parties disappeared. New ones were formed and gradually the political scene began to resemble a two-party system: two competing coalitions vied with each other for the government and the presidency. Elections thus became a participatory link between the people and their government.

Participation did not progress adequately in several areas: the relationship between Parliament and the cabinet; the dialogue between interest groups and the State; the development of an ongoing relationship between the administration and the administered; between workers and managers, and above all, in providing closer contacts between the citizen and the regional, town, departmental and municipal units. No genuine fiscal and administrative autonomy was granted to municipalities and regions and no genuine participation in forming economic and developmental plans was given to the grassroots. France continued to be governed from Paris and by Paris. Yet, and this is not unrelated to the Gaullist period, the demand for participation was strengthened. The number of civic and voluntary associations multiplied, and the imperatives of community control reasserted. The participation of the recipient of services among students, consumers, townspeople, villagers, workers, the retired, farmers and the small manufacturer and the artisan became more pressing. Such participation was often spearheaded by a number of voluntary and professional organizations but also by political parties.

Economic and Social Modernization

In writing Stalin's epitaph, Isaac Deutscher pointed out that he had come to power when the wooden plough was still the symbol of Russia's backwardness, and had died when the country had mastered nuclear technology and was vying with the United States as an industrial power. It would be an exaggeration to make a similar statement about DeGaulle. Yet there would be some truth in it. Most people have associated him with the search for impossible political dreams: rank, world power and a haughty disdain for the economy. But it is not so. DeGaulle, like many French leaders even among conservative ones, had a passion for technology and economic development. "Technology dominates the universe," he wrote. Not only did he consider it an ingredient of national power and therefore felt that it was the role of the State to promote it whenever individual initiative flagged, but he also felt that it was a *sine qua non* for the social and political transformation of France—for an end to the rule of encrusted privilege and the division of the country into warring factions and classes.

For modernization to take place, at least two important factors must appear and develop, each one progressively reinforcing the other. Their combined weight will inevitably affect the political system. First, there must be large-scale industrial organization together with rapid economic growth and massive application of technology to industrial production. Second, there must be a parallel diffusion and consolidation of common attitudes and values. There must take place, in other words, a gradual weakening of differences with the formation of a body of citizens who share common goals and aspirations, and develop common attitudes and values.

Both of these overall factors appeared clearly in France in 1945, immediately after World War II. They gathered momentum throughout the period of the Fourth Republic to manifest themselves fully under the Fifth Republic, which began in 1958. Components of these factors for modernization included:

1. The decline of the petite bourgeoisie—shopkeepers, artisans, small manufacturers, and small farmers—both in numbers and in influence. They gave place to large-scale organizations in industry, commerce, and agriculture.
2. The opening of opportunities to hitherto underprivileged groups, through massive development of educational facilities that became much more widely accessible to all.
3. The broadening of job opportunities so that both the expectation and the reality of upward social mobility were preserved.

4. A common and uniform improvement of living conditions tangible for many groups.
5. A feeling on the part of the underprivileged groups, notably the workers, that social mobility was real, that opportunities were available to them, and that they shared in the fruits of national prosperity. Real wages rose. In addition, the entrance of workers into new technical jobs and the ensuing differences in income blunted the traditional revolutionary militancy of the workers as a class. Further, the influx of immigrant labor for the lowest-paid menial jobs for the first time provided the French worker with a feeling of belonging to the national community from which he had felt separated and by whose leaders he had felt exploited for so long.
6. A cushion against insecurities arising from ill health, accidents, unemployment, and old age. Unprecedented social legislation in France provided to a degree for this cushion.
7. Encouragement for the development of large-scale industrial organizations. The nationalization of key industries such as coal, electricity, gas, transportation, and some automotive firms provided this encouragement to the French industrial class and promoted massive application of technology, especially in aeronautics, railway transport (nationalized in 1937), chemicals, agricultural machinery, energy, and even nuclear power.
8. The direct intervention of the state to provide for credits and establish economic priorities. This was accomplished through economic planning, instituted in France as early as 1946, but also through the direct intervention of the French Civil Service in economic and managerial activities. The traditional French bureaucrat—aloof, neutral, and concerned with the strict application of the law—gave place to a new breed of men and women involved in policy-making and policy implementation with regard to economic and industrial affairs. The distance between the civil servant and the industrial manager, the banker, or the engineer has become increasingly reduced.

The cumulative impact of these changes gradually produced a communality of values and attitudes, expectations and aspirations, and tastes and habits. The new media of communication—notably the advent of television—reinforced it, while large-scale organizations such as supermarkets and chain stores, universities, and vacation and youth centers, provided gradually for a sharing of common opportunities, consumption standards, and common experiences that began to level off the regional and group distinctions. Social classes and regions began to shed their specific "cultures" to merge progressively into one. A new synthesis began to emerge: more cooperative nationally, assertive and dynamic, future (rather than tradition) oriented, seeking pragmatic and rational solutions on the basis of a growing agreement to societal problems.

By 1969, when DeGaulle left office France had, as he had put it, wedded itself to the twentieth century. "Once upon a time there was an old country hemmed in by habits and circumspection. At one time the richest, the mightiest people among those in the center of world stage, after great misfortunes, it came, as it were, to withdraw within itself. . . . Now this country, France, is back on her feet again."[7]

Whatever the factors that helped the recovery of France, DeGaulle and his associates could justifiably take pride in it. Between 1945 and 1970 the population had grown from about forty million to over fifty-two; the per capita income reached over $3,000 to become the highest among the Common Market countries; the productivity of the French worker reached and exceeded that of the Germans; real wages (to which various social security benefits are added) had tripled; the active population began to approximate the profile of other industrialized nations with a rapid decline of farmers (from about 25 percent in 1945 to just around 12 percent in 1970) and the rapid growth of the tertiary sector; urbanization progressed steadily with fewer and fewer French living in small villages and more and more in towns of over 10,000. There are still few large metropolitan areas other than Paris but more than one hundred small cities with over 50,000 and forty-five with 100,000. Free education is available to all. There are more than 700,000 university students—as compared to less than 100,000 in 1945 and the annual examinations for a lycée degree that used to attract not more than 20,000 then was taken by over 300,000 in 1974!

There are, to be sure, still some elements of backwardness. The firms continue to be relatively small. More than a third of the workers work in firms that employ less than fifty workers and the majority is in firms that have between 75 to 175. The distribution sector is still in the hands of small shopkeepers and supermarkets account for only a small percentage of total sales. Marginal units in agriculture subsist, though the use of tractors, fertilizers and modern techniques is rapidly improving the yield per acre to make the French agriculture one of the most productive in Europe. While the merger of firms into larger units capable of competing with those in Germany or Holland and Belgium has been noticeable, there are still too many small ones. Finally there are difficulties in financing and the procurement of credit that has accounted for the slowdown of expansion. Yet with over 5 percent of economic growth annually since 1958, France has led the way in Europe. Unemployment has hovered between zero to about 1.5 percent at a time when more than a million and a half foreign workers have been attracted to the country, occupying the menial and poorly paid jobs, in mining and industry, now disdained by the more prosperous French workers.

FOREIGN POLICY

World War II, despite its victorious outcome, was a record of bitterness for DeGaulle. The fate of Europe was decided by the Russians, the Americans and the British. France was unable to intervene. The alliance with the United States in the form of NATO in 1949 after DeGaulle had withdrawn from the political scene became France's sole security. The defense of Europe was virtually in American hands. Thus when France appeared on the road to recovery after her liberation, world developments underscored her weakness and her dependence upon a friendly but foreign power.

This was the situation when DeGaulle returned to power in 1958. While there was never any doubt that American protection was needed, and that Soviet Communism represented the obvious danger for Europe and France, he was determined to break away from American tutelage and to assert fully France's independence and freedom of action. The course he had to follow was a difficult one. In essence he had to oppose a friendly but overwhelmingly powerful ally—as long as the potential enemy did not threaten. He had to steer a careful course between the ally's threshold of tolerance (which he knew to be high) and the enemy's potential aggressiveness (which was considerably moderated with the death of Stalin and the subsequent emergence of the Sino–Soviet dispute).

Immediately after his return to power in 1958 DeGaulle asserted in a memorandum addressed to President Eisenhower, Prime Minister Macmillan and Henry Spaak, Secretary General of NATO, that it was not the intention of France to limit its foreign policy "within the confines of NATO." It is, however, common knowledge that the memorandum was a diagnosis of the problems facing NATO and, in addition, a statement of French policy. DeGaulle indicated his sympathy with the common responsibilities imposed upon the alliance in case of war, but pointed to the inequality in military strength and, furthermore, the inequality in the power to make decisions among the allies. He proposed, therefore, the establishment within NATO of a "directorate" of three—Britain, France, and the United States—with the responsibility for elaborating a global military and political strategy, creating allied commands for all theaters of operation, to say nothing of joint strategy deliberations and decisions for the use of atomic weapons. "The European states of the continent," he stated on April 11, 1961, "... must know exactly with which weapons and under what conditions their overseas allies would join them in battle." He pointed out that "the theaters of war are no longer limited to Europe" and that the North Atlantic Treaty Organization should accordingly be revised to meet jointly non-European problems. There was also a threat in the memorandum: France would reconsider its NATO policy in the light of the response of Britain and the United States.

Since the allies seemed unwilling to subordinate use of atomic weapons to a "directorate," France proceeded with the explosion of its own atom bomb in 1960 and with preparations for developing and testing hydrogen weapons. Several additional reasons for so doing were then given: the uncertainty about the use of the bomb by the United States except in self-defense; the need for a French deterrent; the injection of a new pride and higher morale in an army that had experienced one frustration after another; and finally, the worldwide commitments of France.

As long as other powers have nuclear weapons, DeGaulle argued, the only policy consistent with French interests was to develop nuclear strength. And at the various disarmament conferences the French continued to favor the liquidation of stockpiles and delivery missiles *before* the suspension of the manufacture and testing of nuclear weapons.

While opposing European political integration, DeGaulle was quick to use as a political weapon the hopes of his partners that the Common Market might lead to an eventual political union. In 1963 he decided that Britain, whose ties with the United States appeared to him too close, should not be permitted to join the Common Market. He concentrated on establishing special relations with West Germany and repeatedly stated that political cooperation in Western Europe should be based upon intimate relations between the two former enemies. When the successor of Konrad Adenauer, Ludwig Erhard, appeared to hesitate and then to favor continuing close ties with the United States, DeGaulle opened up the prospect of direct negotiations between France and the Soviet Union to settle the future of Germany. In the meantime he continued to whittle down France's participation in NATO until in 1966 he announced his decision to withdraw from it (but not from the Atlantic Alliance) and requested the withdrawal of all U.S. power from the French soil. The recognition of China, his trip to Latin America in 1963, his pronouncements in favor of the "neutralization" of Southeast Asia, his criticisms of "military and political intervention in the affairs of other states" (during the American intervention in Santo Domingo in May 1965), his scornful rejection of the Moscow Test Ban Treaty, were all part of the same grand design. France under DeGaulle was an independent world power.

Yet there is one part of the Gaullist legacy that relates to some crucial problems the French are facing. DeGaulle undermined one of the most cherished dreams of post–World War II Europeans. He was an obstacle to European union, refusing to promote the establishment of European political union. His passionate desire for independence led him to reject what he professed to espouse—a European "whole." His nationalism should have been European, aiming at the creation of Western European independence, which was feasible and realistic in terms of its power configuration, rather than French national independence, which was something of an illusion.[8]

But even with a united and independent Europe there would remain the problem of what DeGaulle called "Europe's daughter"—the United States. The majority of the French, even if they prefer a Western European union independent of the United States and an independent European Third Force, still see in the Atlantic ties and in the presence of American troops in Europe the ultimate guarantee of France's and Europe's security. A large majority realize that the American deterrent is France's ultimate defense. DeGaulle's defiance of American policies, his decision to break away from NATO, and to consider defense as an exclusively national affair could have resulted in a situation in which France would have made American support to Western Europe difficult or—even worse—divisive. The alternative policy, according to many critics, was to cooperate within NATO while trying to build a united Europe with Britain and to try within the councils of NATO to press for greater equality, consultation, and division of labor with regard to theaters of operation and matters of overall strategy. France's policy should ultimately be directed toward an independent Western Europe allied with the United States. DeGaulle's purpose—the full independence of France able to assume the leadership of Europe to become a Third Force or a "balance" in world politics dominated by the United States and the Soviet Union—was doomed to failure.

ENDNOTES

1. DeGaulle, *War Memoirs* (New York: Simon and Schuster, 1960), Vol 1, p. 3. This volume describes DeGaulle's efforts in the beginning of World War II to create a resistance movement against Germany, to bring the Empire to rally behind him, and to persuade the allies to give him recognition and support.

2. Ibid., p. 320.

3. For a more detailed account see my introduction to *DeGaulle: Implacable Ally* (New York: Harper and Row, 1966). Also Stanley Hoffmann, *Decline or Renewal: France Since the 1930's* (New York: Viking Press, 1974), pp. 283–442.

4. P. Williams and M. Harrison, *Politics and Society in DeGaulle's Republic* (New York: Doubleday; Anchor, 1973), p. 204.

5. For a full development, see Roy Macridis and Bernard Brown, *The DeGaulle Republic: Quest for Unity* (Homewood, Ill.: The Dorsey Press, 1961); and Williams and Harrison, *Politics and Society in DeGaulle's Republic,* pp. 203–242.

6. For a fuller discussion see Pierre Avril, *Politics in France* (London: Pelican, 1969), Ch. 4. Chapter 2 gives a number of Gaullist precedents followed by Pompidou.

7. *Major Addresses, Statements and Press Conferences of General Charles DeGaulle, May 19, 1958–January 31, 1964,* N. Y. French Embassy, Press & Information Services, p. 79.

8. For a different point of view, Hoffmann, *Decline or Renewal,* pp. 283–442.

chapter two

The Pompidou Years (1969-1973): Gaullism Without DeGaulle

DeGaulle's years were years not only of achievement but of challenge. Challenge to the world in the name of national independence; challenge to the Europeans to close ranks behind France and form a power bloc to offset the weight of the superpowers; challenge to the French old political class and parties to abandon their old ways and ideological quarrels, but challenge also to the monied and business interests to modernize the economy, to acquire technology fast and apply it to industrial production; and, finally, challenge to the nation to move out of its rigid compartments, classes and hierarchies into a modern, homogeneous and consensual society. Long before Jean-Jacques Servan-Schreiber, a maverick progressive political aspirant, had written *The American Challenge*[1] in 1967 to show to his fellow citizens the tasks ahead when confronted with the realities of American industrial power, DeGaulle had thrown France's hat into the ring where only industrial giants were supposed to compete.

In contrast, Pompidou's years were years of consolidation and, some say, even of retreat. Pompidou himself struck the tone in announcing his candidacy, after DeGaulle's resignation on April 28, 1969, when he admitted that he could not (nobody could) be as great a man as DeGaulle. All he could hope was to be a little "less great"! His task was unenviable; he knew that every one of his acts and every one of his decisions would be compared with DeGaulle's. The French with their passion for historical analogies went back to the years after Napoleon when nobody talked about anything else but the demise of the great man. Others compared Pompidou and his period to the Orleanist years (1830–1848), when the revolutionary spirit and the Napoleonic glories gave place to a government by the upper bourgeoisie, timid and selfish, entrusting the reigns of government to a small group of men of affairs, lawyers and notables, unable to generate leadership and shying away from direct contacts with the masses of the people. With Pompidou, some said, France threw away her Gaullist spurs in exchange for slippers; others regretfully remarked that France gave up the brilliant and sometimes expensive game of poker DeGaulle played for quiet nights of gin-rummy.

The Pompidou years, however, are too close to us to allow any such sweeping generalizations and comparisons. DeGaulle's France had lived for over ten years under a personal presidential system in which the discretion of a man was tempered by individual and public freedoms and by four legislative elections and five referendums. It was precisely Pompidou's problem to institutionalize and to legitimize the Constitution of the Fifth Republic, which had been so closely associated with the "charisma" of one man. Would the institutions remain intact? Would presidential government continue to provide for an accepted instrumentality of government? The first section of this chapter attempts to answer these questions. The second section will relate to foreign policy: What were the continuities and discontinuities in France's foreign policy under Pompidou? The last section examines briefly the economic and social policies.

Pompidou and the Political Institutions

During the electoral campaign of May–June 1969 for the presidency, Pompidou made it clear that he was committed to continuing the institutions of the Fifth Republic but also to an "opening." He planned to improve the relations between the Executive and the legislature—especially the National Assembly—and between the Executive and the "majority." He was ready to consider reducing the presidential term from seven to five years, but otherwise he didn't contemplate any constitutional reforms or any qualifications of the presidential powers. Once elected he considered himself the national spokesman, the guarantor of the institutions and the liberties of the French, the incarnation of national sovereignty—a "guide" responsible for major policy orientations and decision-making.

PRESIDENTIALISM

We noted that DeGaulle's Constitution differed from DeGaulle's interpretation and practice. The Constitution had divided the Executive into two: the President and the Prime Minister with his cabinet. According to Article 20, the cabinet derives its authority from the confidence of the National Assembly and "shall determine and direct the policy of the nation." In 1959 a theory was developed according to which there was a "reserved domain"—notably in defense and foreign policy—that came under the President. Soon, however, this theory was abandoned in favor of presidential dominance. The duality of the Executive—between the President on the one hand and the Prime Minister and his cabinet on the other—gave place to a hierarchical relationship with the

President on top and the Prime Minister and the cabinet as his subordinates. But even this was further qualified to reduce the Prime Minister and the cabinet to the mere role of implementation—with the President's office directly assuming the responsibility of policy-making. Presidentialism under Pompidou, despite the promise of an "opening," crystallized into direct presidential government. The Gaullist heritage was kept alive; indeed, it was strengthened. Here are the great lines of the theory and the practice of presidential government:

1. Pompidou continued to claim to incarnate the national sovereignty by virtue of his direct election by the whole nation. The President is not only responsible for the broad policy guidelines but for their execution as well.
2. The Prime Minister owes his authority and his position to the President and derives his powers not from the Constitution or the confidence of the National Assembly, but from presidential designation. He is the President's man and can be removed by the President at will. In May 1972 Prime Minister Chaban-Delmas, received an overwhelming vote of confidence in the National Assembly only to be removed from office within a few weeks by Pompidou.

   Both DeGaulle and Pompidou speculated on the relationship between the Prime Minister and the President. Their conclusions are remarkably similar: there ought to be a harmonious relationship between the two. Within the broad context of common policy guidelines, shared by both, the Prime Minister has freedom and discretion. However, being in charge of everyday problems and policy execution he is expendable. The political climate may change, and there can be calls for a new Prime Minister with a new cabinet. Underlying these facts there are some equally important political realities that have not been mentioned:

   a. The Prime Minister, if allowed to established himself firmly in the National Assembly with majority support, may become a rival to the President instead of remaining a subordinate.
   b. If it is the policies of the President that are unpopular, then the Prime Minister becomes a convenient scapegoat —leaving presidential authority intact.
   c. There may be one majority in Parliament supporting the Prime Minister and another in the country supporting the President. In such a case outright dismissal gives the President the opportunity to refashion the parliamentary majority and align it to the presidential one without having to resort to dissolution of the National Assembly and a

new election. Pompidou was the first President to entertain this possibility by indicating that even if his Prime Minister were to lose on a vote of confidence in the National Assembly, the President was not bound to dissolve and call for an election. He could call upon another Prime Minister. This, he pointed out with pride, showed the flexibility of the French Constitution giving full discretion to the President to cope with changing political situations.

3. Pompidou strengthened the Gaullist practices regarding the relations between President and cabinet and reinforced presidential dominance. First, cabinet members continued to be appointed and dismissed by the President—with only the *formal* consent of the Prime Minister. Pompidou appointed his own men in crucial ministerial posts and removed others. Second, and more important, he intervened directly with the individual ministries for the purpose of imposing his own policy, vetoing projected policies, or taking matters away from the cabinet and making them part of presidential policy. Often this was done in the cabinet meetings over which he presided. But it was not uncommon for the President to send a direct communication to a minister, thus by-passing the Prime Minister. The relations between the French President and his cabinet resembled relations between the American President and his cabinet, who hold office at the President's pleasure.

4. The similarity with the United States presidency does not stop here. There was also a parallel growth of the "office" of the French Presidency. A select group of civil servants assisted the President in formulating policies and often in supervising their implementation. With responsibilities that often paralleled those of the Ministries and with special assignments to elaborate policies, they were not only the eyes and the ears but also the brain and the nervous system of the President's office, linking it with the rest of the Executive branch: the Prime Minister, the cabinet, the nationalized industries, the Planning Commission, and the administrative agencies. The "office" became progressively institutionalized and bureaucratized with a commanding role in policy-making. The President's staff consisted of persons who came from the same select schools, had held administrative posts before and aspired to political or administrative advancement. They were intimately associated with civil servants who worked also in the Prime Minister's office and who staffed the various Ministries. The "administrative class" as a whole formed and continues to form a network of communications between the President's office and the offices of the various Ministries

that further undermines both the autonomy of the Ministries and the independence and control of the individual minister.

To illustrate the dominance of the presidency under Pompidou: in his last two years in office, he

1. dismissed his Prime Minister to appoint a new one;
2. intervened directly in the selection of the Speaker of the National Assembly;
3. proposed a constitutional reform on condition that no amendments be allowed.
4. requested his Minister of Finance—Valéry Giscard d'Estaing—to abandon the chairmanship of the political party he headed—the Independent Republicans;
5. intervened directly in the proposed legislation to reorganize the Radio and Television Office;
6. hand-picked the Secretary General of the Gaullist party and later when one of the faithful party lieutenants failed to be selected in the party's executive committee, he made him Minister of the Interior;
7. proceeded likewise to designate some of his closest associates or prospective supporters to ministerial jobs;
8. undermined and vetoed his Prime Minister's policy with regard to regionalization and participation.

These illustrations do not include matters of defense and foreign policy that were personally conducted by the President. He often surprised the cabinet and his Prime Minister by announcing policies and proclaiming directives that had not been debated. Pompidou was just as Gaullist as DeGaulle. DeGaulle had asked the United States forces to leave France and severed his relations with NATO by sending a communication to President Johnson and the NATO allies that was "discussed" in the cabinet three days after it had been sent out! Pompidou agreed to Britain's entry in the Common Market after a long personal talk with the British Prime Minister in the summer of 1971.

Under Pompidou, cabinet stability remained high. There were two Prime Ministers in just five years as compared to three in DeGaulle's ten years. Almost the same stability for the Ministry of Foreign Affairs (two incumbents), the Minister of Finance (one incumbent), the Ministry of the Interior (two incumbents), but also the same relative instability for Education, Housing and Equipment, Social Affairs. Many of the ministers hailed from the Gaullist era, including his two Prime Ministers. But gradually supporters of Pompidou and leaders of his presidential majority moved into the scene. In contrast to the Gaullist early period where many ministers were technicians and civil servants, most ministers came from the National Assembly. Many of them, however, had been newcomers to politics and had sought and secured a seat in the National Assembly *after* they had served as ministers or at top administrative positions. They were "imposed" upon the electorate from the top rather than coming up from politics into ministerial positions. Only in the last year did Pompidou revert to the Gaullist practice by designating his ministers of Foreign Affairs and Cultural Affairs from outside the National Assembly.

There were frequent reshufflings of the cabinet—twice under Chaban-Delmas (1969–1972) and four times under Messmer (1972–1974). But with the exception of one they were relatively minor ones. Often the same individuals remained in the cabinet but changed posts. A hard core of about ten kept the key posts—Foreign Affairs, Defense, Interior, Finance, Justice. A total of about sixty shifted from one position or another to account for the full complement of a cabinet that averaged about thirty-four posts (including undersecretaries). The leadership remained stable; changes were made in the periphery or in particularly sensitive spots. Cabinet discipline was maintained with occasional sharp exchanges between rival ministers that became increasingly sharper as the health of the President began to fail.

THE LEGISLATURE

Despite promises made by Pompidou to improve relations between the Executive and the legislative branch, the Parliament continued to be the "orphan" of the Fifth Republic. One reason was that Pompidou inherited in the National Assembly an overwhelming majority committed to him. At least 290 Gaullists, 60 Independent Republicans and some 33 centrists (Progress and Modern Democracy) rallied to him during the presidential election. More than 380 deputies out of a total of 490! Only the Communists, the Socialists and a group of centrists refused to rally: they formed the "opposition." In the only two motions of censure against the Prime Minister that were introduced between 1969 and 1973, there were only about 95 deputies to vote against the government. It was a "majority" that was supposed to be taken for granted. In fact, it was ignored. Major bills and government proposals were discussed by the newly instituted "liaison committee of the majority" consisting of the leaders of the three political parties that had supported the President. The parliamentary committees were bypassed or were not given the time and the opportunity to examine government bills; the urgency procedure was often used; the government had often to resort to the "blocked vote" rejecting all amendments and forcing a vote on its own bill. More than 85 percent of all laws enacted were introduced by the government.

In 1971 the dissatisfaction of the parliamentarians in the National Assembly reached a high point. The chairmen of the legislative committees, mostly Gaullists, communicated their strong dissatisfaction to the government. They complained that the Parliament was not given the time and the opportunity to exercise its traditional functions of control and deliberation; that the urgency procedure was being abused; that government bills were not accompanied by the appropriate supporting documents and that in effect legislation was decided at the governmental level and by the "liaison committee of the majority" so that the National Assembly had become a rubber-stamp. They further pointedly argued that the government was far more sensitive to interest groups and their spokesmen than to the Parliament. They concluded somewhat anticlimatically that "a bad conception of executive-legislative relations" prevailed. For the first time, the legislature was attempting to reassert its role as a body without, however, transcending the limitations imposed upon its role by the Constitution. Within the constitutional boundaries it had a role to play but was not given the opportunity to play it.[2]

Not until 1973, however, after the legislative election, did the National Assembly begin to reassert itself. This was due partly to the strength of the opposition—there were now about 210 votes ranged against a reduced majority (about 270)—but partly also because the majority itself began to show signs of divisions. Pompidou reverted to the Gaullist stance by continuing his Prime Minister in office without soliciting a vote of confidence. The National Assembly riposted by introducing two motions of censure against the Prime Minister in a period of less than one year—just as many as had been introduced in the previous five years. The last motion, introduced on January 24, 1974, was voted by 208 deputies.

The President also suffered a number of defeats. His constitutional reform to reduce the President's term to five years didn't receive adequate support. He decided to withdraw it rather than submit it to a referendum. A bill introduced by the government regarding veterans' pensions was amended against the government's desire, and the government was forced to withdraw it. The measures to promote decentralization were frequently amended both by the National Assembly and by the Senate. The limits of presidential dominance over the legislative branch were becoming increasingly apparent while the future of executive-legislative relations remained unclear. The authors of the authoritative annual political and economic survey, the *Année Politique*, summed up the situation as follows: "By the end of the parliamentary session (December 1973) it appeared that the link between the majority and the government had weakened. The cleavage that had emerged previously, Opposition vs. Government, gave place to a certain degree to a new one . . . between Legislature and the Executive. . . ."[3]

POMPIDOU AND THE "MAJORITY"

Presidential dominance derives in great part, as we have seen, not from constitutional powers and prerogatives but from the existence of a loyal "majority" in the National Assembly to support the Prime Minister and cabinet, or, in other words, to support the President himself. However, it is not a question of a party majority. Even since 1958 the "majority" was a coalition of parties and groups. Only between 1968–1973 did the Gaullist party have an absolute majority in the National Assembly. Pompidou and his government could have governed in this period by relying exclusively on the Gaullist party. Many orthodox Gaullists urged the President to do so and to ignore the latecomers and outsiders whose fidelity was questionable. Pompidou refused and decided to rely upon all groups and parties that had supported his election. He preferred a presidential coalition.

The reason lies in an inherent contradiction between party government and presidential government that is likely to affect the future as well. The President does not wish to be the spokesman of a party—no matter how strong; he would rather be the national spokesman. A strong party with tight organization and leadership may inevitably become a restraint upon his freedom to act and govern. A strong majority party is also likely to generate a strong and united opposition that can challenge the President and his government. The "flexibility" of presidential politics will give place to rigidity, partisanship and a high degree of polarization. The French President like the American one has no desire to create a strong party machinery, with a good organization and clear ideological commitment. It may overshadow him. There is a tendency to choose "coalitional" rather than party politics, so that the base of the President's support remains constantly fluid with a "majority" whose contours are unclear. It is an elastic and open majority replenished by newcomers to compensate for the possible losses and always open to outsiders.

But even if the President attempted to form or to rely upon a highly disciplined party it might be impossible to create it. Even if France has moved progressively from ideological and bloc parties in the direction of large coalitional groupings, residual ideological, social and class divisions are ever present. Some such divisions and conflicts within the Gaullist party as well as between the Gaullists and the rest of "the majority" were still much in evidence and they continue to be important. Running as a presidential candidate, Pompidou made every effort to gloss over these differences. He campaigned on concrete issues. He favored continuity, stability, a dialogue with all forces and groups. He promised reforms where he thought reform was needed. France would continue a policy of independence but in cooperation with its traditional allies; he would take measures to decide on the future of European unity; he would reconsider Britain's entry into the Common Market; efforts would be made to reimburse the refugees from Algeria for their losses; educational reform would continue, but without undermining the authority of the teacher; the franc would be defended; planning would continue in consultation with all interest groups and parties; every effort would be made only to arrest inflation but without disregarding the legitimate demands of the wage earners, and so forth. Ambiguity was calculated to enlarge the presidential majority and to avert conflicts within the Gaullists.

There were at least five divisions within the Gaullist party representing factions that often overlapped on some issues and divided on others. First and foremost there were the Epigones—the faithful *compagnions* of DeGaulle who by virtue of their long fidelity and service considered themselves the designated heirs. They had no desire to merge with the other groups or be a part of "the majority"; nor did they have high regard for Pompidou, a latecomer. As soon as Pompidou became President some groups that had embodied various aspects of Gaullist orthodoxy emerged. The Association for the Presence and Action of Gaullism, under one of the Gaullist leaders and the Gaullist party organization—the *Union de Jeunes pour le Progrès*—was committed to social reform. The same reformist orientation was expressed by many of the deputies as well. New groups were founded, such as the *Association for the Social Contract* under the Speaker of the National Assembly. Individual Gaullist leaders began to present their views against the Prime Minister and even the President.

A second division was the Gaullist "Jacobins" fighting against the Gaullist "Girondins." Here fidelity to DeGaulle seemed to inspire both sides. The "Jacobins"—headed by the first Prime Minister of the Fifth Republic, Michel Debré, with powerful support from former ministers and parliamentarians—were against anything but the most superficial measures of administrative decentralization. The "Girondins," reviving the old tradition of federalism in the years of the French Revolution, stood for regionalism. They were led by Chaban-Delmas, a faithful Gaullist.

Third, there were the "technicians"—pragmatic, service-oriented, with a managerial outlook that occupied a dominant position in the new regime, against the "politicians"—whose career had started at the grass-roots level before they moved up to the National Assembly and to ministerial posts with an eye to votes, public opinion, interest groups and prone to conciliation and compromise.

Fourth, the Gaullists were divided—to borrow the term of a French political scientist—into the "party of order" and the "party of movement." "Movement" meant a propensity for reform and change, a desire to do away with old structures and vestigial economic and social units. "Order," on the other hand, is the equivalent of status quo—a tendency to maintain the existing balance of social and political forces, to find the most feasible common denominator, to respond to each and all of the interests present and preserve them. At least half of the Gaullist deputies elected in the landslide of 1968 represented "order."

Finally, there were the "Europeans," who were committed to a genuine European Community with independent powers as opposed to what we may call the "nationals." The "nationals" paid lip-service to European Community as long as it served French interests—especially agricultural interests—and as long as Europe was to be primarily a consultative arrangement involving no impairment of national sovereignty.

The lack of any genuine leadership allowed these various divisions to fester until the Gaullist party became progressively demoralized. Three secretaries-general succeeded each other between 1969 and 1973. In their meetings and study groups the Gaullists united in supporting the President but remained at odds on almost everything else. In the Gaullist Party Congress of Nantes, in November 1973, the orthodox Gaullists were able to win the majority of the Central Committee and to elect a person as secretary-general who was hostile to the Prime Minister. A number of Pompidou's men were ousted. The revolt was aimed at the internal leadership of the party and was made with an eye to the President's failing health and hence the forthcoming presidential election. It was also directed against the "men of order" and their immediate allies, within the "majority"—the undesirable "cousins" who had been invited to the Gaullist table, notably the Independent Republicans and their leader Giscard d'Estaing.

A strong party or a presidential coalition? This remains the crucial and unresolved issue. The Gaullist party—after purging itself of some of the more conservative elements—promised organized support. It proved capable of mobilizing the voters and of creating a tight government front based upon close links between the majority in the National Assembly, the Prime Minister and the President. Pompidou opted for the "majority," that is, a coalition of all those who supported him and the formation of a cabinet that represented them. It gave him flexibility; the power to blunt the demands of the reformists and the orthodox Gaullists and to claim that he was not the prisoner of any political party but the spokesman of a wide spectrum of opinion.

This, together with the President's failing health, was the reason for deteriorating relations between the government (and the President), on the one hand, and the National Assembly, on the other. The Gaullists, even when they had an absolute majority between 1969 and 1973, became restive. They began to act in the Assembly as a party should: they introduced amendments, refused to give their support to government measures, and insisted on being the party with a privileged relationship with the government. In response the government resorted to some of the procedural practices of the past—the urgency motion and the blocked vote forcing the deputies to fall into line. After the election of 1973 the position of the Gaullists in the National Assembly hardened. Pompidou's reluctance to go along with social and administrative reforms, the manner in which he had dismissed his Prime Minister, but also his efforts to support his own lieutenants rather than rely upon the orthodox Gaullist leaders, produced a growing hostility on the part of many of the Gaullist members in the National Assembly. This hostility was sometimes directed against the President but more often against his Prime Minister and more particularly the Minister of Finance—Giscard d'Estaing—who, it was rumored, was the President's choice to succeed him.

POMPIDOU AND THE PUBLIC

Pompidou continued the Gaullist practice of communicating directly with the press and the public at large. Three major methods were used: 1. the press conference, 2. the televised addresses, and 3. special visits to the provinces. There were also direct communications to the Parliament, special press releases, and occasional meetings with parliamentarians and leaders of the Gaullist party and of the "majority." As with DeGaulle the public was kept daily informed of presidential activities and declarations. They began to expect and to demand presidential statements on virtually all policy issues.

The Press Conference

Pompidou held regular bi-annual press conferences in which after an introductory statement of general policy he answered questions for more than an hour and sometimes longer. Under DeGaulle the questions were assembled in advance and sometimes "planted" or even contrived, so that DeGaulle could speak his mind on what he cared to develop most. With Pompidou there seemed to be no prior restraint upon the newspaper correspondents. Scandals, pending legislation, constitutional questions involving the relations between the President and his Prime Minister, the length of the President's term, the relations between the President and cabinet members, the evaluation of electoral results and trends, were all covered frankly and sometimes in detail. The same was the case with foreign policy questions.

The Televised Address

Two kinds of televised addresses were used: the formal annual assessment of the year's activity with the President's New Year wishes, and the ad hoc ones addressed to a particular problem. The latter assumed a particular importance in weeks preceding the legislative election or the referendum. Pompidou addressed the nation twice prior to the legislative election of 1973—the second time only 24 hours before the balloting (when campaigning was legally closed). Similarly the President addressed the nation and made speeches in several of the provincial capitals during the referendum of April 1972, calling for the entry of Britain into the Common Market.

Visits to the Provinces

Pompidou continued the Gaullist practice of visiting the centers of the various regions of France. DeGaulle had visited all of them. Pompidou was not given adequate time to do so, but he proceeded very much along the same lines. During two-day trips he was accompanied by some of his advisers and cabinet members; receptions were held in the prefecture of the departments where the *préfet,* the deputies from the departments, the mayor, and other public servants received him; a speech followed sometimes with luncheon or dinner. The overall purpose was similar to the various visits of the American President, though the occasions were more formal and structured: to appear before the people, to make contact "with the masses" and to maintain or create the personal link and, hopefully, strengthen his support.

Without attempting to discuss Pompidou's "charisma," there is no doubt that he remained popular. Opinion polls gave him consistently a positive rating. It remained fairly stable at about 53–56 percent, following a curve that never reached the heights of DeGaulle's but which also never experienced the occasional negative ratings DeGaulle had experienced.

THE REFERENDUM

In the Gaullist system, as we have seen, the referendum was more than a request for the approval or the rejection of a policy question. It was a plebiscite: the approval or disapproval by the whole nation of the President. "You are for me and my policy," "I ask for your expression of confidence," "I demand your massive and decisive vote in favor of my work." These were some of the expressions that DeGaulle had used to urge support of the policy measures he submitted on five occasions before the people. Pompidou felt also that presidential government should be buttressed by occasional appeals to the nation, but he used the referendum only once. He, too, asked for a frank and massive vote in favor of the measure he submitted, which was not without ambiguities, as we shall see when we discuss foreign policy questions in our next section. But either because of the issue chosen, or because Pompidou did not stake the fate of his own presidency upon the results, he failed to get a positive public response. More than a year later, he was faced with the only alternative of submitting his proposal for reducing the term of the presidency to five years to a referendum, and he decided not to call one.

Thus, since the fateful "no" to DeGaulle in 1969 only one referendum has been called—and it failed to buttress presidential leadership. It is quite likely that future Presidents may be tempted to abandon the practice rather than to endanger their position; or, they might resort to it but only after they eliminate all personal and plebiscitary traits. In other words, the prospects for the future may well lie in the "Americanization" of the referendum or rather in its use in strict accordance with the French Constitution.

Foreign Policy

In 1944, after military defeat and prolonged occupation of their country, the French were asked in a survey whether France was still a great power. Eighty percent answered yes. Throughout the Fourth Republic, the French political class remained faithful to the vocation of greatness. DeGaulle, when he returned to power in 1958, did not innovate. He favored independence and a great power rank. Not a shred of national independence was to be sacrificed to integrative schemes— military, economic or political. The Common European Market was accepted as a convenient scheme for economic cooperation. The Atlantic Alliance was considered necessary but not its integrative military arrangements. The army was reorganized in a manner that emphasized the primacy of the nuclear weapon—with improved delivery capabilities and the development of some four nuclear submarines with missiles. France stood alone with the possibility of deploying the weapon against anybody "from wherever he came," as General Ailleret announced in 1967. The "opening to the East" became a cardinal move in DeGaulle's diplomacy during his last years as President. The aim was to establish better relations with the Soviet Union and make American military presence less imperative but also to convince the Soviet Union to relinquish its hold over Eastern Europe.

When Pompidou came into office the Gaullist aspirations had not materialized. On the contrary, it seemed that the basic Gaullist design —to create an independent Europe under French leadership and protection and to undermine the Soviet position in Eastern Europe and the American position in Western Europe and to prevent a Soviet-American cooperation that he equated with a "condominium"—had failed. Even the remarkable industrial growth in France and its strong economic position in the world declined dramatically in 1968, following two months of revolutionary uprisings that left the economy crippled. DeGaulle's only definite and irreversible success was liquidating the war in Algeria; the French officer corps returned to France, together with about 400,000 draftees and about a million French citizens who lived there.

Would Pompidou take a new look at the situation to change the major guidelines that had inspired DeGaulle? To do so he would not only have to go against the Gaullist legacy but also against the aspirations of the French who had approved it. We shall examine the foreign policy under Pompidou with regard to the Common Market and Europe, the Atlantic Alliance, the Franco-Soviet relations, and the evolution of French strategy. First, we shall briefly discuss presidential dominance as it applies to foreign policy.

PRESIDENTIALISM AND FOREIGN POLICY

Continuity with the Gaullist practices was the rule. The President alone made foreign policy. His Secretary of Foreign Affairs reported directly to him and implemented presidential directives. The Prime Minister played only a secondary role. He remained informed, although sometimes after the decision had been made. Pompidou met personally with the leaders of other countries. He hosted the Soviet leaders twice and visited the Soviet Union twice. His last visit abroad, only a few days before his death, was in the Crimea. He held bi-annual meetings with the German chancellor; hosted the Queen of England in the spring of 1972; and had frequent meetings with the British Prime Minister. He had three special meetings with President Nixon, including a visit to the United States. He toured virtually every part of French-speaking Africa. Despite his ill health he visited China. Personal and direct diplomacy became the common practice for everything except some technical economic matters involving the Common Market.

The form corresponds to the substance of foreign policy. Decisions are made by the President and his staff. He alone decided after meeting with Prime Minister Heath to "reverse" the Gaullist policy and admit Britain into the Common Market; he alone decided to put this before the people in a referendum; he launched the European Summit Meeting in Hague in 1969 and initiated a second Summit in Paris in 1972. In his last months in office he attempted to recreate European political cooperation rather than submit to the American "designs," as outlined by Henry Kissinger in his London address of December 1973. He also refused any permanent and structured pattern of consultations between the United States and Europe about the oil embargo.

The President relied upon the advice of his associates. But the impulse came from him. Presidential dominance was just as real as it was under DeGaulle. But Pompidou appeared, at least until his last year in office, more modest in his aspirations. The Gaullist challenges to the world were replaced by more practical considerations in which economic motives predominated. How to get oil; how to improve the position of the French farmers in the Common Market; how to establish economic cooperation with the Soviet Union; how to maintain Franco-American relations without flaunting American power or American policies in faraway areas (Vietnam or Latin America or Canada). No major new policies were outlined or suggested—except for enlarging the Common Market, to which we shall return. Incrementalism was the rule with Pompidou continuing by and large the Gaullist lines but qualifying them as time went on in the light of changing international events and in terms of a more realistic appraisal of France's power and influence in the world. The aspiration became more modest in line with the realities of French power; but the assertion of "independence" as opposed to entangling alliances remained just as strident as under DeGaulle.

FRANCE AND THE COMMON MARKET

The ultimate goal of the founders of the Common Market (an economic union involving reduction and elimination of tariffs among the Six, creation of a common tariff for all and the gradual elimination of all impediments to free movement of labor and capital but also the positive equalization and harmonization of economic policies and practices, be it wages, social security measures, taxation, interest rates, and so on) was political union. They expected that ultimately decisions would be made by a qualified majority vote and that a European executive—the Commission—and a European Parliament would begin gradually and in specified areas to make decisions binding upon the member states. The ultimate dream of the founders was to establish a federation of European states with common political institutions endowed with supranational powers. Pompidou as a candidate for the presidency ran as a European and it was widely rumored that he favored not only stronger European ties but also the inclusion of Great Britain in the

Common Market. He was considered also to have a far more realistic appraisal of DeGaulle's foreign policy. Only *in* Western Europe and *with* Western Europe (that is, the Common Market) could France become again a center of power. But what kind of Europe was it to be? And what would be the relations between such a Europe and the United States, the Soviet Union and the rest of the world?

Three major European summit conferences in Hague in 1969, in Paris in 1972, and in Copenhagen in 1973; innumerable meetings between the ministers of the six Common Market countries and a referendum on "Europe" in April of 1972, are the major landmarks in terms of which we can assess Pompidou's policy and objectives.

The Hague Conference (December 1–2, 1969)

In the Hague conference Pompidou presented the famous triptych for the future of the Common Market: *achèvement, approfondissement* and *elargissement. Achèvement* meant the completion of the financial agricultural arrangements to create a common agricultural market with an external tariff and a complex procedure of price controls and subsidies to farmers. It benefited the French farmers and was constantly declared by the French officials as absolutely necessary for the consideration of all other economic and social matters. *Approfondissement* meant the "development in depth" of the Common Market to cover banking and monetary policy, harmonize taxation, equalize social security legislation and establish some political machinery through which Europe would speak "with one voice" in international affairs. *Elargissement* meant the expansion of the Common Market by including other states—notably Britain—as full members.

It was a challenging presentation but the question of priorities was left unsettled. Would development in depth come before expansion? Pompidou opted for the broadening of the Community, and the inclusion of Britain, Ireland, Denmark and Norway. But when the Common Market partners urged the strengthening of the political integrative institution by giving more powers to the Executive Commission and to the European Assembly, Pompidou demurred. He was willing to allow for the rapid exploration of means to "develop in depth" the Common Market towards a monetary union, the establishment of a common patents office, and harmonizing taxation. But he opposed any form of political integration. Throughout his presidency this remained the dominant theme of the French. They continued to do everything within their power to undermine the development of community political institutions that could even remotely affect, let alone override, French sovereignty. Pompidou never went beyond the Gaullist position of favoring periodic meetings among the heads of states and their Foreign Ministers. He recommended establishing a Political Secretariat of the member states to be located in Paris in order to coordinate information, prepare studies and facilitate a common deliberation of foreign policy questions.

The Referendum of April 23, 1972

In January 1972 the four candidate members of Britain, Denmark, Ireland and Norway were admitted into the Common Market in a treaty that had to be ratified in one form or another by the Common Market countries and by the new member states. "Having assumed personally the responsibility for this," stated Pompidou in his Press Conference, "first in Hague, then in my meeting with Prime Minister Heath (summer of 1971) and having authorized the signature of the Treaty, I consider both my duty and in accordance with democratic principles to ask the French people, who have elected me . . . to express themselves directly on this European policy."[4] The referendum was to be held on April 23, 1972, and was to be followed by a new European Summit meeting of all the members of the Community, including the new ones.

The question before the French voters was two-fold: 1. the approval of the Treaty enlarging the Community, and 2. the overall approval of Pompidou's European policy. In a clarifying document to all French voters it was stated that they had to decide whether Europe would move progressively toward a confederation that would preserve the personality of the states that comprise it. In an earlier press conference Pompidou had speculated on the future of Europe. "The construction of Europe is possible and necessary," he said. "But what kind of Europe? . . . There can be no other way than to create a confederation on the basis of what we have, namely a confederation of states that agree to harmonize their policies and integrate their economies. But to do so there must be a government whose decisions are binding upon the individual states. It is an illusion to think . . . [that a confederation] . . . can emerge from specialized and technical committees and commissions."[5] In the meantime a "European government" had to be based upon the individual governments representing individual and sovereign states acting through their spokesmen.

To some people confederation was contrary to the Gaullist heritage; to others Pompidou was not going far enough toward a genuine political Europe. The matter was further confusing because of the strong national overtones that accompanied the call for the approval of Pompidou's foreign policy: it would serve French interests; promote France's strength; consolidate her independence. Opinion was divided. The Communist party had urged a "No" vote. The Socialists counselled abstention. The centrists voted yes because they wanted European Union and favored the entry of Britain but opposed Pompidou's lack of willingness to go beyond vague phrases about a confederation. The results were disappointing for the President. For every hundred registered voters only thirty-seven voted yes; seventeen voted no and the rest abstained. It was a defeat, especially when we compare it to the current polls in which more than 70 percent of the French favored Britain's entry.

How sincere was the French President in outlining the prospects of a European confederation? Only a month after the referendum he toasted the Queen of England during her state visit. "The deep-rooted sentiment of our national identities," he said, "shaped throughout many centuries . . . [will not] . . . be dissolved in a purely technical and economic conglomerate." To which the Queen answered, "The forces of Europe have been weakened by national rivalries."[6] Throughout the subsequent monetary crises that were soon to bedevil Europe and the relations between Europe and the United States, the French held fast to the propositions that all questions should be handled by the Ministers of Finance of the individual states.

The Paris Conference (October 19–20, 1972)

The summit meeting of the nine European countries (Norway decided not to join the Common Market), represented by their top political leaders, took place to consecrate the entry of Britain, Denmark and Ireland into the European Economic Community, but also to face up to some new and urgent monetary problems and to consider the reform of its institutional structures.

The Nine (Britain, France, West Germany, Italy, Belgium, Holland, Luxembourg, Denmark and Ireland) constitute a formidable economic, trading, industrial, financial, and potentially even military bloc. They comprise two hundred and fifty million people, with about 40 percent of the world's trade. They produce more steel and more automobiles than the United States and the USSR, respectively. They account for about 50 percent of the world's merchant marine, and enjoy a standard of living that ranks among the highest. Two of the countries (Britain and France) have mastered nuclear technology and have nuclear arms. Six of them have gone through almost fifteen years of close cooperation, which brought important tangible and even more important intangible benefits: a common agricultural market and a common external tariff, the elimination of internal tariffs and trade barriers, massive and intensive cultural exchanges. The way had been opened for preparing some genuine integrative plans: a European common monetary system with perhaps even a common currency and a European bank; social and welfare harmonization; regional planning and regional development within a European framework; reciprocity to all educational degrees; free mobility of capital and labor. The Six had also streamlined their institutions into one Executive—the Commission and a European Parliament. However, little progress had been made in establishing some kind of institutional arrangement that stops short of a genuine federation but is something more than a loose confederation. The time for a political Europe had come.

Two courses for creating a political Europe were open to the European leaders who met in Paris: either to expand the role and functions of the Common Market institutions—the Commission, the European Parliament, and the Council of Ministers—and empower them to deal with political questions or to establish what in effect amounts to a "two-track" Europe—an economic Europe operating under the existing Common Market arrangements and a new political Europe with new institutions. An "economic" Europe at best meant continuing and gradually extending the status quo. The nine states would attempt gradually to coordinate behind a common tariff internal economic matters in an effort to "harmonize" their domestic economies. But assuming that the Common Market, and notably its executive Commission, moved toward harmonizing and coordinating taxation, social legislation, minimum wages, banking, and money—even to the extent of envisaging the creation of a European bank and of European currency, its powers would remain limited.

Yet there is still an element of supranationality in the provisions setting up the European Community. The Treaty allows for a qualified majority in the Council of Ministers. It has been explicitly incorporated in the amendments associated with the entry of Britain and the other countries in the European Community. Within the Council of Ministers, Britain, Germany, France, and Italy have ten votes each; Belgium and Holland five each; Denmark and Ireland three each; and Luxembourg two. The requisite majority is forty-three. It has been the hope of the "Europeans," many of whom had to abandon reluctantly their more ambitious federalist plans, that a political Europe could be set up by broadening the jurisdiction of the European community so that political questions would come ultimately under the qualified majority rule. The French have insisted, however, that "whenever there are important interests involved the discussion must continue until there is unanimity." The national veto remained the rule.

The summit conference failed to reach an agreement on the political future of Europe. A number of economic problems were discussed and some decision reached. The French insisted on a European monetary union or at least a commitment to go ahead with it. It will not be "completed" until December 31, 1980. The word "completed" (*achève*) is never defined to mean what it should; that is, by that time, if not sooner, *all* European currencies would be treated as a unit in their fluctuations vis-a-vis all outside currencies. Ambiguity and studious delay were the rule when it came to institutional reforms and political cooperation. There was nothing except the expression of pious hopes for cooperation in developing a common foreign policy. Nothing specific was decided on how to establish a common dialogue between the Nine as such and the United States. Lip service, to be sure, was paid to the need of consultations, but even the idea of a European political secretariat was discarded. What is more, nothing was said about common defense and strategy and the relations of the Nine within or without NATO. As for the reform of institutions, it was simply agreed to proceed with studies for the strengthening of the "powers of control" of the European Parliament. The question of its election by universal suffrage was sidestepped. The conference also agreed to study the prospects "of transforming before the end of the present decade and *with the fullest respect of the Treaties already signed* the whole complex of relations of member states into a European Union." By 1975 a report is to be prepared and submitted to a new summit conference.

The Summit at Copenhagen (December 14–15, 1973)

The European summit meeting in Copenhagen in December 1973 was called because of a series of circumstances that urgently required common decisions: the situation in the Middle East, relations between Europe and the United States, and the energy crisis. Each of these items was related to economic and political but also to strategic developments that had placed France and Europe into severe difficulties. None of the hopes associated with the establishment of European institutions had materialized. Crucial monetary difficulties—the devaluation of the dollar, the reevaluation of the Deutsch mark, the uncontrolled fluctuations of European currencies, the constant pressure on the part of the United States for commercial and trade arrangements to take into account the U.S. military expenses in Europe (evaluated at $3 billion a year), strong divergencies among the European states with regard to Israel—all of them had undermined the spirit of European cooperation. Europe remained politically an entity consisting of nine relatively small sovereign states.

At this juncture Pompidou and his Foreign Affairs Minister, Michel Jobert, rose belatedly to support European solidarity, the search of a European identity, and an effort to define it and to give it its own defense. "The Nine affirm their common will to see Europe 'speak with one voice' when it comes to worldwide matters." The Conference adopted a declaration stressing the following:

1. The understanding that all bilateral arrangements made by the Nine should take into greater consideration the common positions agreed by them;
2. The chiefs of states should meet more frequently;

3. The specific character of the European entity should be respected;
4. The institutions of the community must function fully and rapid decisions must be made;
5. The relations between the Commission, the Council of Ministers and the European Parliament should be improved in order to expedite decisions but also to reinforce the budgetary control powers of the latter.

We must then conclude that despite the overt professions of Europeanism, there was no tangible evidence in Pompidou's policies that France had relinquished its stand against any political integrative arrangements in Europe. The ruling body remained the Council of Ministers and the individual veto of each of the countries comprising the Common Market reemphasized on a number of occasions. A political Europe endowed with some representative institutions that can speak on behalf of the Nine is still to be made. In this sense Pompidou remained as Gaullist as DeGaulle. The French insistence on national independence and freedom of action in foreign policy and defense remain the major stumbling block to European integration.

THE ATLANTIC ALLIANCE AND DEFENSE

Two basic propositions have shaped French foreign policy and defense. First, that the division of the world into two "blocs," under the respective control of the United States and the Soviet Union, is unacceptable; second, that in our nuclear world possession of nuclear weapons is the only corollary to national independence. Hence, no integrative alliances should be made that qualify a country's freedom to act.

These two propositions have diametrically contradictory implications when they apply to the United States—the leader of the Atlantic world—and to other states, particularly in Europe, that do not have the nuclear weapon. In the first case France's position is a call for independence against the United States; in the second it is a call for the dependence of the European states upon France for their protection and makes France (or at least so it is hoped) the leader of the Western European nations. This contradiction has made European unity impossible and has also marred relations between France and the United States.

The French "revolt" against the United States[7] (dating from the first exchanges between DeGaulle and Roosevelt) has taken every conceivable form: political, economic, cultural, diplomatic and strategic. Powerfully supported by the Gaullists and the Communists (for different reasons) this defiance of the United States position and rule has been popular among the French. It has led to the withdrawal of France from NATO and the unwillingness to consider permanent consultative relations between the Common Market and the United States. The French never agreed to participate in a disarmament conference. They claimed that it was designed to keep the monopoly of nuclear weapons among those who already had them. They refused to participate in the negotiations for a balanced and mutual reduction of forces in Europe, anticipating a deal between the Russians and the Americans that would weaken the defense of Europe. And they of course have had nothing to do with SALT (Strategic Arms Limitation Talks). They have protested against the agreement for preventing nuclear war signed by the United States and the Soviet Union in the summer of 1973—because they were not consulted but also because they feared a lowering of the American commitment to defend France and Western Europe.

To France's European allies its position is incompatible with their interests. First, any effort to undermine the Atlantic Alliance means that their own defense will be weakened; secondly, whatever reservations they have about the United States posture—diplomatic, monetary or strategic—they feel that they should be expressed and negotiated by a united Europe (which the French have opposed). They are willing to proceed with strengthening the European institutions provided that France accepts their logic and submits to common decisions. Finally, they are unwilling to explore a common European defense, except on the basis of a common and genuine pooling of forces and in the context of the Atlantic Alliance.

In 1973 it was primarily the effort made by the United States to develop a new Atlantic charter and reassert the solidarity of the Atlantic world that provoked strong French reactions. They saw again in the United States efforts a design to "control" and dominate Europe. When Secretary of State Kissinger remarked that the European identity cannot be defined and expressed outside of the Atlantic whole he was repeating what in effect most European leaders, except the French, had argued. Nor was Kissinger implying that such a "compatibility" between Europe and the United States and the other members of the Atlantic Alliance called for United States domination. He was seeking a structured pattern of consultations. At this point Pompidou reverted to the Gaullist hard line by calling for independence of Europe, the acknowledgment of a European identity, the need (conceded until then by all other members of the Common Market but France) to develop the proper political mechanisms so that Europe could speak with "one voice," and finally the need for developing a common European defense. It represented a return to DeGaulle's foreign policy.

But it was France's concept of defense and its strategy within the Atlantic Alliance that created even more serious problems. To begin with, former Secretary of Defense Robert McNamara's doctrine of graduated deterrence first announced in 1961 forced French strategists to reconsider their defense policy. Graduated deterrence would allow for a possible confrontation of the superpowers *in Europe* giving them the freedom to test each other's will and intentions at the risk of bringing doomsday upon the old continent, while preserving their respective national sanctuaries. This was deemed, and rightly so, to be contrary to France's independence and survival. The first reaction to the McNamara strategy was to substitute French massive retaliation for the American one! The trouble was that it was not massive enough, that it could not be quite as credible and that it also carried unacceptable risks for many of France's allies in Europe as well as for the United States. French strategists therefore were forced to reconsider. They have tried to develop a theory that attempts to reconcile the Atlantic Alliance with the French nuclear force.

The new strategy is a "how to have the Alliance and the bomb" strategy. To put it in a nutshell, the French were willing and indeed expected to use the Atlantic Alliance *as a first line of defense* against an aggressor (everybody seemed to agree again that the aggressor was likely to "come from the East") but also to maintain France's untrammelled freedom to use its nuclear force in the last resort. The argument of the French strategists runs as follows: supposing there is an aggression from the East—then the Alliance becomes operative and the NATO and French forces together engage the aggressor on the basis of the existing bilateral arrangements, presumably somewhere in Europe. If, however, during these forward operations it becomes clear to the French leaders that the aggressor is *aiming* at France's territory, that his *intent* is indeed to occupy France or destroy it or seriously imperil its vital interest France then will be free to act alone, by using its nuclear forces. At this point the so-called *critical threshold of aggressiveness* is reached (to be determined, however, by the French leaders). This is where the French can and will communicate to the aggressor through appropriate but unequivocal signals their readiness to use their nuclear weapons and to use it if the aggressor fails to respond appropriately. All cooperative arrangements in other words that may exist between France and the Alliance are set aside in favor of French unilateral action the very moment the French leaders decide that the critical threshold of aggressiveness *for France* has been reached. A nuclear retaliatory strike will presumably follow against the aggressor irrespective of what the allies do and even if they are still engaged in battle.

This appeared to be the French position under Pompidou. It was contrary to the inherent logic of the Alliance. It is hard to see which allies can agree and how they can accept to engage their forces in common against an aggressor while simultaneously leaving to the discretion of one of them the freedom to jeopardize and indeed to literally destroy the whole in the name of its vital interests. Why should France's allies act as France's first line of defense unless there is a common strategy which protects their own forces and interests while protecting France? Why should they go along in a common effort that threatens the existence of their own forces by putting them at the mercy of one of them?

The nuclear force without solid and integrative alliances is isolating France—both from the United States and from its European allies. No genuine European defense can be developed without genuine pooling of military resources and a common plan of how and where and by whom such resources will be used. Similarly no strong European defense is possible without the American deterrent which means deciding how the European forces will be related to those of the United States and the other members of the Atlantic Alliance and how, where, and by whom they will be used. The French have been unwilling to consider a European integrated force and have withdrawn from the integrative military arrangements of the Atlantic Alliance.

This is perhaps the greatest weakness of the French position today; it is the most unfortunate part of the Gaullist legacy and one to which scant reconsideration seems to have been given until now. Without integrative military alliances—and without a political Europe that can elaborate a common strategy and defense—without NATO but also without the desire to seek new integrative alliances, France is faced with the prospect of increasing rapidly its conventional forces at high cost or of emphasizing its independent national nuclear capability and thus of moving even more to a purely defensive posture that will underwrite its isolation. In the last analysis, France cannot rely upon its nuclear force without strong cohesive and integrative alliances, yet it cannot make integrative alliances without abandoning the grandiose and rigid emphasis upon military and nuclear independence.

RELATIONS WITH THE SOVIET UNION

Pompidou continued to follow the guidelines laid down by De-Gaulle. Frequent consultations between the leaders of the two states were held; economic arrangements were negotiated (representing, however, only a modest increase in the trade between the two countries). The truth was that with the occupation of Czechoslovakia by the Russian troops in the summer of 1968, the last efforts on the part of France to provide an "opening to the East" based upon a withdrawal of Soviet political and military control there had failed. There was little that the French could give and even less that the Russians wanted. Furthermore, all claims on the part of the French diplomacy to be the leader in an "opening to the East" and to improve East-West relations became irrelevant with the new German Ostpolitic which resulted in treaties between

West Germany, the Soviet Union and the Eastern European countries, new arrangements in Berlin, diplomatic recognition and normalization of relations, and above all prospects of economic relations between West Germany and Eastern Europe, including the Soviet Union, that the French could not provide.

In the growing world of détente, the French under Pompidou had even less to give. With the withdrawal of the French forces from NATO but the continuation of the Alliance there was little that could change the status quo. In the last year of the Pompidou presidency the remarks made by the French President and his Minister of Foreign Affairs about a Soviet-American "condominium," and more particularly an independent European defense, were sharply criticized by the Soviet leaders. Since there is no prospect for France to trade off her Atlantic Alliance with a different one, there is very little that France can do to arouse genuine Soviet interest and support. The Gaullist strategy of using the one side against the other cannot be successful when the two superpowers manage to reach direct agreements to maintain the status quo.

CONCLUSION

Continuity of the Gaullist policy under Pompidou seems to have been the rule. Even when he admitted Britain and the other two countries into the Common Market, the French President was not altering the course of French foreign policy. In the last year of the Gaullist presidency there were intimations that DeGaulle was prepared to do the same. Fearful of the success of political integrative mechanisms, disenchanted with the failure of the Franco-German treaty of 1962 to lead to a strong Europe under the joint leadership of the two (but with France having the nuclear weapons), DeGaulle had begun to lose interest in the Common Market of the Six and to favor a looser arrangement with other European states including Britain.

The policy vis-a-vis the Arab world and against Israel has remained the same. Every effort was made to maintain relations with French-speaking Africa and to improve them with Northern African states—Tunisia, Morocco and Algeria. Nuclear tests continued and the nuclear weapon was improved but its credibility remains as precarious as before. And despite some efforts to establish an understanding with NATO on technical strategic matters, the independence of France's nuclear posture and unilateral strategy was maintained. Within the European countries France has refused to participate in the Euro-group, which provided for standardization of weapons and military procurement in the context of the Atlantic Alliance and in cooperation with it. While joint projects with European states succeeded—such as the Concorde, for instance—no agreement was made on a common nuclear energy policy, with the Common Market countries splitting into two groups. France under Pompidou became progressively isolated. The desperate search for a role in world affairs had brought no tangible results. In the name of national independence and non-alignment France found itself more and more alone.

The Society and the Economy

When Pompidou came to office France was still in the wake of the uprisings of May–June 1968. It was a period of constant unrest among university and high school students, artisans and shopkeepers, workers, truck drivers and farmers. Modernization and improved living conditions had whetted expectations and raised demands—for greater security and for higher wages, for protection of vested interests, for subsidies and supports, for consultation and participation. But it aroused a sharp debate about the social goals of industrialization and economic expansion. While Pompidou and his associates never questioned what had become known as the "industrial imperative," that is, the need of industrial expansion and growth, many among the intellectuals, some of the left-wing parties and some of the trade unions began to subordinate it to social and qualitative requirements: security, leisure, improved conditions of everyday life, education, culture, and above all the elimination of sharp income inequalities. Many people demanded the freedom to control and decide for themselves—in the factory, in the universities, in towns and villages—instead of allowing an impersonal and highly centralized state to make decisions for them. The French men and women began to reject the tutelage of the centralized administrative state and to yearn for what we call "community control."

It would be difficult to say that even tentative answers were given to these questions during the Pompidou years. It was a period characterized by a great disparity between promises and realizations in the social domain, a continuing economic and industrial growth that benefited most socioeconomic groups, but of only timid and incremental social and administrative reforms.

THE "NEW SOCIETY"

Even before his election Pompidou had agreed to ask one of the leaders of the Gaullist party, Chaban-Delmas, to become Prime Minister. In exchange the Gaullists gave their full support to the President. The Prime Minister, however, began by striking out on his own with ambitious plans for social, economic, and institutional reform—to launch what he called the "New Society."[8] His overall program was based upon an analysis of the state of the French society and a set of proposals to reform it. According to the Prime Minister, the French society remained "blocked."[9] The economy was still fragile. Despite industrial growth there were still too many farmers, too many small firms, too many marginal and relatively unproductive small units. The standard of living was still low. Rapid industrial development to provide a stronger economic base for the country and more jobs was indispensible. This required not only continuing economic expansion that all Gaullists advocated but also rapid concentration of industrial firms, elimination of unproductive and marginal units, elimination of marginal farms, increase of capital investment in industry.

His program also called for decentralization; for reducing the powers of what he called the "octopus state" (*état tentaculaire*). Its responsibilities had increased rapidly and the whole society had come under its domain. It was solicited by all for protection and subsidies but also for reform in all areas of social life. Local units suffocated; the nationalized and public services had lost all autonomy. It was time to break up the monster by providing for genuine regional and local autonomy and initiative and by allowing public and private units and associations the freedom to experiment and to reach decisions desired by the individuals concerned. It was time to give to the trade unions and the managerial groups a sense of their responsibilities as well as freedoms by asking them to decide together on policy matters of mutual concern. A "contractual society" should replace the administrative and hierarchical one that still existed. The Prime Minister pointed out also that the French society remained a "society of castes." Great differences of incomes still separated social groups and classes and there was not enough upward social mobility. The solution lay in the rapid improvement of salaries and of opportunities—including professional training for the workers; in a growing dialogue between trade unions and the corporations; in the expansion and improvement of educational opportunities for all; and in liberalizing the means for information and culture so that state agencies like the radio and television service could be at the disposal of all.

The "new society" was a challenging indictment of the Gaullist state. It was not likely to please the men of "order" in the majority and even less so the centrists and the Independent Republicans. But neither was it likely to appease the left, which saw in the Chaban-Delmas proposals nothing but an effort to steal some of their thunder and their votes. The "new society" was not pleasing to the "bureaucracy" or to the managerial groups and the head of the corporations. But above all it was not agreeable to the President himself.

The "new society" never came into being! Only some incremental reforms were made and others initiated. Some were vetoed or delayed by the President himself; others by sometimes the tacit and sometimes the overt collusion of the President and the majority. When Chaban-Delmas brought the matter to a head by asking with the grudging consent of the President a vote of confidence in the National Assembly —which was overwhelmingly given—his fate had been sealed. In July 1972 a new cabinet under the leadership of Pierre Messmer was formed. He was one of the orthodox Gaullists. Messmer had been Minister of Defense for many years under DeGaulle but had shown little interest in fundamental reforms. He was likely to be more the President's man than was Chaban-Delmas, who had a popular base and a party base. Between July 1972 and March 1973 when the legislative elections were held, reform was set aside in favor of stability; change in favor of consolidation.

Incremental reforms were all that came out of the program for a "new society." A special program was established for the "professional formation" of workers (in marginal economic activities) and of women. The remuneration of workers on a monthly basis—which provides for greater security and a better social package—was instituted, but it could not be extended to all categories of workers and firms. The "contractual" policy resulted in stable agreement in many of the nationalized industries and was supported by the Trade Union. Finally, social and economic measures were introduced to provide for an increased minimum salary, better social security measures and better retirement benefits. But there was no administrative reform, no genuine effort to modify the structures of the State and diminish its empire over the society and the economy. Long debates and controversies did not result in giving anything approaching autonomy to the radio and the television service. No genuine effort was made to liberate the university from State control and to provide for a more egalitarian and open system of education; no reform of the secondary education was undertaken. Above all, no regional "decentralization" was introduced. Minor reforms were enacted but they left the local units under the control of the State.

Industrial growth continued, however, at the rate of about 5.5 percent a year—the highest in the Common Market countries. Despite inflation, real wages increased by at least 35 percent between 1969 to the end of 1973. Only about 750,000 workers remained at the minimum monthly wage level of about $160, while the average basic wage rose to $410 a month in 1973. In addition, profit-sharing began to be used more widely. For instance, in 1971 about two million workers received

$72 each. More fortunate were the workers in some chemical and pharmaceutical firms who received $140 each. Full employment was maintained, though there were some indications that hidden unemployment existed in some areas. Despite price controls, inflation remained endemic. It averaged about 7 percent a year before it went almost out of control in 1973–74 when it rose over 14 percent.

Despite the combination of industrial growth and increase in the gross national product with the rising real wages, the rising expectations of many of the salaried accounted for an ongoing social crisis throughout the Pompidou years. The year 1971 was a year of continuous social upheaval. In 1969 some two million and a quarter days of work were lost because of strikes; the figure doubled in 1971. The trade unions reached an agreement on their specific demands—increase in real wages, improvement of working conditions, guaranteed employment and better retirement benefits—and pressed for the promised policy of contractualism, demanding that agreement be negotiated between their representatives and the employers. Employers were unwilling and the government was reluctant. The result was a constant series of strikes—among the farmers, who asked for guaranteed higher prices or for freedom to raise their prices; the workers, in both private and nationalized industries; the artisans and the small merchants who asked for increased social security benefits and who were against the new supermarkets; the truck drivers, the winegrowers, the students both at the university and the high schools; the foreign workers who protested their dismal living and working conditions; the employees of banks, the professors and teachers, and on and on. At times even the police were affected, and on one occasion the judges demonstrated.

Time after time the trade unions, despite their many ideological conflicts, presented a common front and gave the same directives to their members. The Communist-dominated General Confederation of Labor, with about 1,600,000 members, the French Confederation of Democratic Labor, with over 700,000, the "Force Ouvrière," whose membership had been reduced to less than 500,000, but also the Federation of National Education with about half a million members: all joined ranks not only on specific claims but at times on political issues as well, thus reviving the practice of a political strike. This prompted the Prime Minister to state that the decisions of the electorate could not be "modified in the streets."

In 1973 President Pompidou and his government seemed satisfied with maintaining the status quo and at the same time continuing rapid industrial growth. Perhaps the vast changes that France had undergone in one generation after World War II were all that a society could absorb; perhaps a period of consolidation or even retreat was needed.

Despite the promise of a "new society," it was a society a little more like the old one that Pompidou left to his countrymen. There was the familiar trend to reestablish a balance between the various socioeconomic forces; to reach a new synthesis in which the various economic groups, through their political spokesmen, would have their vested interests protected. In a new economic context, in a far more prosperous country the trend in favor of protection rather than change was reasserting itself, as it had under the Third Republic. The perennial resistance to change had been overcome for a given period of time. But now again a convergence between old interest groups and new ones that had emerged was manifesting itself in favor of protection and the status quo. The bureaucracy, the farmers, the new managerial groups, the industries that were subsidized by the State, but also the farmers, the shopkeepers, the artisans, the trade unions and the associations that spoke for the interest of managerial firms, joined forces. The French society seemed "blocked" once more. The mentality for protection and subsidies and guarantees rather than innovation and change affected not only the Gaullists but also the Left, notwithstanding their rhetoric to the contrary.

ENDNOTES

1. First published in France in 1967, *Le Défi Americain,* Denoël, 1967. Published in the United States under the title of *The American Challenge,* trans. Ronald Steel (New York: Atheneum, 1968).

2. *Année Politique,* 1971, Presses Universitaires de France, Paris, pp. 66–68.

3. *Année Politique,* 1973, p. 124.

4. *Année Politique,* 1972, p. 216.

5. *Année Politique,* 1972, p. 232.

6. *Année Politique,* 1972, pp. 241–242.

7. Stanley Hoffmann, *Decline or Renewal: France since the 1930's,* pp. 332–362, "Perceptions and Policies: France and the United States."

8. For an account of the "New Society" program with excerpts from the major speeches by Chaban-Delmas, see Jean Bunel and Paul Meunier, *Chaban-Delmas* (Paris: Stock, 1972).

9. For a general discussion Michel Crozier, *The Stalled Society* (New York: Viking Press, 1973) and Stanley Hoffmann, ed., *In Search of France,* (Cambridge: Harvard University Press, 1962).

chapter three

The Evolution of
the Political Forces:
The Legislative Election
of March, 1973

Introduction

The economic changes that occurred after the liberation of France by General DeGaulle, pursued during the Fourth Republic and continued after the Fifth began to have their impact upon the French political culture. These changes affected political orientations, attitudes, beliefs and values and, lastly, the character and organization of the political parties and the party system as a whole. Several indications of change were present long before DeGaulle returned in 1958. People became progressively disenchanted with weak and shortlived governments which were incapable of translating their aspirations into policy. They also became tired of a multiparty system that led to coalition cabinets and made it impossible for the voter to choose a government on the basis of programmatic declarations. The French public began to favor executive leadership and presidential government as opposed to legislative supremacy with a weak Executive. There was a growing estrangement from the institutions of the Fourth Republic. There was also a great deal of instability among the parties—some of which declined rapidly while new ones were formed—until in 1958 with DeGaulle's return the new Gaullist Party (UNR—Union for the New Republic) began to gain ascendancy over the others. It formed a coalition with other parties to become "the majority," as it came to be called.

But on the left too there were signs of regrouping. The old Socialist party declined rapidly. It was not revived until 1971 when a number of political clubs and associations, headed by François Mitterrand, advocating a united left formation in cooperation with the Communists, infiltrated it and captured its leadership. The Communist party, too, began to gradually change its ways in seeking a broad cooperation with all anti-Gaullists, and especially the Socialists. In the process the Communists had to reconsider their most cherished ideological commitments: class war and the dictatorship of the proletariat; the prospect of participating in a government; the abandonment of revolution and of the outright socialization of the means of production.

The second ballot of the presidential election of 1965 indicated the beginning of a genuine regrouping of the political parties with the Communists, the Socialists, and a fraction of the centrists voting for Mitterrand and the rest for DeGaulle. It was also the beginning of what became known as the "Gaullist phenomenon" or, better, the "majoritarian phenomenon." But even earlier the Gaullists with their allies from the right or the center had won a majority in the National Assembly in the legislative election of 1962. This in turn forced the left-wing groups to strengthen their cooperation. In the subsequent legislative election of 1967 and again in 1968 they ran their individual candidates on the first ballot but supported each other on the second and often crucial ballot. In 1967 the Left—or the "opposition"—almost managed to dislodge "the majority" by receiving 240 seats out of a total of 487. The June 1968 election was called by DeGaulle in the wake of the student and worker uprisings that paralyzed the French economy, brought the Gaullist State to the brink of collapse, and frightened the middle classes. There was a noticeable backlash and the Left lost. The Gaullist "coalition" emerged victorious with more than 370 deputies out of 487. The Gaullists *alone* had a majority.

This defeat of the Left together with some persistent doctrinal misunderstandings between Socialists and Communists accounted for its disunity in the subsequent presidential election held in May–June 1969 which Pompidou won. The Left ran their own candidates but was unable to close ranks on the second ballot. The Communists counselled abstention, the Socialists backed a centrist, and Pompidou won overwhelmingly. But this was the exception to the general patterns of regroupings and coalitional politics. Within a matter of two years the Socialists and the Communists reformed their alliance and developed a "common program of government," formally signed in the summer of 1972. Meanwhile, the Gaullists appeared to strengthen their position by continuing to attract to their ranks some of the centrists that had remained hesitant.

France began to assume more and more the profile if not of a two-party system at least of a two "coalitional-party" system. As this evolution became increasingly noticeable, some of the most venerable concepts associated with the study of the French political system began to undergo critical examination. They related primarily to the Left-Center-Right distinction in terms of which political parties and attitudes had been sorted out; to the role of class and ideology in French voting and the strength of partisanship, that is, attachment of the voters to a political party. We shall go over them before we discuss in more detail the legislative election of March 1973 and the subsequent presidential election of May 1974.[1]

Left-Center-Right

The famous dividing line between Left and Right—the French Revolution—finally seems to have been obliterated. The Republican regime, parliamentary and representative institutions, civil rights, religious freedoms, and equality are fully accepted today. But also during the Fifth Republic, the Marxist concept of class and the inevitability of class struggle and revolution have been fading away. So are the basic divisions regarding the Constitution, with the Left favoring legislative supremacy and the Right favoring executive authority and leadership. To be sure, differences remain, but they are usually differences about concrete issues. Even here, attitudes and voting about these issues cut across the traditional Left-Center-Right ideological boundaries. For the first time it would seem that the French public has broken off its old ideological moorings and is floating into unchartered waters.

In his essay, "Paradoxes of the French Political Community,"[2] written in 1962, Stanley Hoffmann, after discussing the socioeconomic factors of modernization in France, refers to a "political lag." Not only political structures and institutions but also the political culture itself had failed to modernize. Political parties remained out of step with public opinion. Participation, while high at elections, remained limited with regard to all other decision-making processes and institutions. According to Professor Beer a modern polity[3] is one that is partisan and participatory in its policy-making; corporatist and technocratic in its power structure; and collectivist in its economic and social policy spheres. It is participation and partisanship (both in the form of well-organized mass parties and of political activity and initiative at local, regional, and associational levels) that France lacked and may still be lacking. However, party developments indicate a clear trend toward modernization. So does the development of participatory mechanisms —from the presidential elections by direct popular vote to local grass-roots involvement, and from bargaining at the highest level on social and economic matters to participation in economic planning down to the regions and departments and localities. The parties are becoming more national and more "aggregative." They are becoming "catch-all" parties; that is, they appeal to all groups and interests.

THE WANING OF CLASS

To the extent to which "class" was ever a significant factor for party identification and voting, it is losing the saliency and the weight it had in the past. Until 1973 only a minority of the workers voted for the Left. In the presidential election of 1969, for instance, out of every 100 workers voting, 32 voted for the Left (the Communist and Socialist candidates); another 32 voted for the Gaullist candidate, Georges Pompidou; 25 voted for the centrist candidate; and 11 voted for the remaining candidates. In the legislative election of 1967, 30 out of every 100 workers had gone to the Gaullists; 18 to the Socialist coalition; 31 to the Communists; 11 to the Center; and the rest were scattered.

This point is reinforced by examining the distribution of Gaullist party voters by socioprofessional categories before 1973. Though Gaullists were slightly underrepresented (compared to national averages) in large towns and among workers, they hovered so close to the national averages that their electoral clientele were a faithful image of the nation in terms of class, occupational, and geographic distribution. The Gaullist vote correlated more closely with the composition and distribution of the population along geographic and socioeconomic lines than that of any other party. While the deviation between the socioeconomic profile of voters and that of the French population was 5.1 percent for the Communist party, 3.2 percent for the Center, and 2 percent for the Socialist coalition groups, it was only 1.5 percent for the Gaullists. Their major deviations corresponded to religion, sex, and age.

THE WANING OF IDEOLOGY

Deutsch, Lindon, and Weil, in a pioneering study[4] attempted to determine the most significant indicators that distinguished Left, Center, and Right. They chose five indicators of a Left-Right cleavage and compared them to the attitudes of persons identifying themselves with Left-Center-Right. If the "extreme Left" and "moderate Left" are grouped together on the one hand and "moderate Right" and "extreme Right" on the other, the responses show that the "indicators" are losing their importance. With regard to the "authority of the state," 25 percent from the Left indicated that it should be reduced and 10 percent had no opinion. On the Right 55 percent favored its maintenance; 28 percent were not particularly anxious to see its authoritative traits reduced; and the rest had no opinion. On the matter of the *école libre* (in fact, subsidies to Catholic schools) the Left voters favored the elimination of subsidies by 40 percent, but 45 percent were opposed and the rest expressed no opinion. The Right was of course overwhelmingly in favor of continuing subsidies. Forty-six percent of those on the Left felt the large private industries ought to be nationalized, but 32 percent of them opposed this move. On the Right side 26 percent favored nationalization, and 24 percent had no opinion. To the statement "Every effort must be made to establish socialism," about 75 percent from the Left gave their assent, as did 35 percent from the Right. Eight percent from the Left disagreed with the statement but only 25 percent from the Right were similarly opposed. Some 36 percent from among the Right did not even express

TABLE 3-1

Opinion	Socialism	Communism	Capitalism
Very good	11%	6%	0%
Good	20	6	5
So-so	21	14	18
Bad	7	21	20
Very bad	2	18	21
None	39	35	36

an opinion. No wonder the authors concluded that Left and Right—indeed all political families—seem to be permeated to an unanticipated degree by common attitudes so that none of them has a fixed and separate position in an ideological constellation.

Nothing illustrated this consensual trend better than the question regarding people's opinions about economic systems—the source of the basic ideological and class confrontations in the past. To the question "What is your opinion of the following economic systems?" the answers were as shown in Table 3-1.

In addition, the opposition between Gaullists and Communists did not appear to the public to be as divisive and fundamental as some might have assumed. To the question "In your opinion is Communism 'opposed' or 'in accord' with Gaullism on the following points?" the answers are as indicated in Table 3-2.

More than one out of two respondents either didn't see any oppo-

TABLE 3-2

	Very Opposed	Rather Opposed	Rather in Accord	Very Much in Accord	No Answer
Foreign policy	7%	25%	39%	6%	23%
Social progress	16	34	25	2	23
National-izations	13	25	21	4	37
Institutions of the Fifth Republic	26	34	7	1	32
Income policy	26	29	14	2	29

sition or refused to answer. A majority of those who answered detected no opposition on foreign policy questions. Twenty-five percent thought that the two parties were in accord regarding "nationalizations," as compared to 38 percent who thought they differed. Thirty-seven percent did not care to answer. The sharpest differences related to the institutions of the Fifth Republic, a distinction that has become less important since the poll was taken.

THE WANING OF PARTIES AND PARTISANSHIP

During the Fourth Republic (1946–1958), the appeal of the parties and of their programs declined sharply. The ideological fervor of the World War II Resistance had been shared intensely and deeply in the years after the liberation by not only the Communists and the Socialists but also by the MRP (*Mouvement Républicain Populaire*—a liberal Catholic party which emerged after World War II). This fervor was reflected in an increase in party membership, party activism, and partisanship. As the years passed, however, attachment to parties declined. For instance, in 1944 to the question, "Do you prefer to vote for a man or for a party?", 16 percent said "for a man," 72 percent said "for a party program," and 12 percent had no opinion. However, in January 1958 the corresponding answers to a similar question were 52 percent "for a man," 27 percent "for a party and its program," while 21 percent had no opinion. In January 1973, with DeGaulle out and with the new election approaching, only 24 percent stated that the party was the major reason for deciding on how to vote. Some 39 percent were concerned with the personality of their individual candidates and local problems.

SOCIOECONOMIC VARIABLES[5]

The major socioeconomic variables that correlate with Left-Right voting have been sex, age, occupation, income, residence, and religion. These variables do not provide an explanation for Left-Right voting in 1973, however. For instance, while the Communist and non-Communist Left received 46.3 percent of the national vote in 1973, they received 49.8 percent of the vote of the age groups between 20 and 29; 49.0 percent between 30 and 39; 47.4 percent between 40 and 49; 47.1 percent between 50 and 59; 44.1 percent between 60 and 69; and 29 percent of those over 70. The Left attracted only a minority of *all* the younger groups in the country.

The correlation between income and left-wing voting is equally inconclusive. The poor and the rich vote *less* for the Left. The Left is stronger among the low-middle and middle income groups. Residence is not a crucial variable either, since the left-wing vote seems fairly evenly distributed. There are some notable regional exceptions, as in the traditional Communist strongholds in some of the Paris suburbs. Occupation divides the electorate more sharply, with the workers supporting the Communists and non-Communist Left. But, only in 1973 did a majority of *all* workers vote for the Left, while a majority of *all* other groups went to the Center or the Right. Sex provided for a variance of about 3 to 4 percent, with males in favor of the Left and females in favor of the Right. Religious practices correlate more accurately with voting patterns: at least 65 percent of those who attend church regularly or occasionally vote for the Center and Right. But even religion is beginning to lose the influence it had upon the voters.

ISSUES AND ISSUE-ORIENTATIONS

The "ideological profiles" and "issue-orientations" that divided Left from Right in the past seem to have become increasingly blurred and to have lost their sharpness and saliency. New attitudes began to be shared by all, and as a result divergences regarding issues decreased. The "exclusiveness" of the social and political "subcultures" began to diminish, and permeability became progressively the rule in a growing national and consensual political community. Left and Right began to share attitudes, perceptions, and aspirations which had kept them rigorously apart in the past. Only the extreme Left remained frozen into the posture of revolutionary defiance, and only the extreme Right continued to pay lip service to authoritarian and antirepublican ideas.

Parties and Voters

THE COMMUNIST PARTY

One of the most remarkable phenomena under the Fourth and Fifth Republics has been the stability—notwithstanding a gradual fractional decline—of the Communist party vote. Many contend, however, that while the vote and the label remain the same the party has changed, and that in fact a vote for the Communists has different connotations than it had in the past. From a "government party" under Maurice Thorez in the years immediately after the Liberation, the party moved into opposition with semirevolutionary overtones between 1947 and 1954. After 1956 it began to move out of its self-imposed political ghetto in cooperation with the Socialists and all other "democratic and popular" forces. The party returned to alliance politics, becoming again a "government party," seeking parliamentary strength and a position in the cabinet. In 1973 it ran as a prospective government party within a left-wing coalition.

It is undeniable that the ideological posture of the Communist party has been changing. It is equally clear that its public image has been transformed. After interminable arguments and negotiations with the Socialists, the Communist party finally abandoned its commitment to class struggle and revolution. It has given up the doctrine of proletarian dictatorship and accepted the principle of party and political pluralism —conceding openly for the first time the possibility that once in the government it would have to withdraw in the face of an adverse election. The party has also accepted religious freedom, heeding the example of the Communist party in Italy. It endorsed a highly gradualistic socialism, and in professing friendly relations with all countries it has attempted to answer those who accused it of an exclusive attachment to Soviet foreign policy. Its attitude during the student and worker uprisings of May and June 1968, when it managed so adroitly to direct a revolutionary situation into trade-union channels, solidified its image of responsibility and moderation, reinforcing its claims to become a government party.

The public has been sensitive to these changes in the Communist party. In 1954, 54 percent of the French believed that Communism represented a real danger for France (fascism was considered a real danger by 35 percent). In 1966, however, only 35 percent stated that they would not vote for the Communist party under any circumstances. In 1966, 51 percent agreed that the role of the Communist party since the Liberation had been either "very useful" (9 percent) or "rather useful" (42 percent). But the figure rose to 54 percent in regard to the activities and responsibilities of elected party officials at the local and municipal level. In the same year (1966) 40 percent of respondents (as opposed to 31 percent in 1964) were favorably disposed to having Communists in the government, and 27 percent did not care. Only 24 percent were opposed, and 9 percent did not answer. Forty-two percent of the respondents felt that in the event a Communist regime came to power in France nobody would stand to gain or lose! Finally, 56 percent thought that the French Communist party had in fact changed; 21 percent did not think so, and the rest had no opinion. Among those who thought the party had changed, 61 percent thought it was more open to discussion, 51 percent that it was closer to the main concerns of the French, and 26 percent that it had become more independent. Generally Communists were considered to be devoted, capable, and humane; few considered them dogmatic or fanatic.

In a survey conducted in 1968, 32 percent of the public considered the Communist party to be "a party like all others," while 41 percent thought it to be very different from other parties and 27 percent had no opinion. Only 30 percent felt that if the Communist party came to power it would outlaw the other parties; 36 percent did not think so, and 34 percent had no opinion. Only 27 percent thought that under certain favorable conditions the Communist party would undertake a revolution in order to gain power; 36 percent did not agree, and 37 percent had no opinion. Forty-eight percent felt that the Communist party worked for the well-being of the people, and only 22 percent disagreed. Thirty percent had no opinion. A survey conducted in 1972 confirmed the willingness of the French to see Communists in the government. But while 48 percent were favorably disposed to seeing Communists in the cabinet, 44 percent and 54 percent respectively were opposed to having a Communist as Prime Minister or President of the Republic. On the eve of the election of 1973 59 percent indicated that they wouldn't object to seeing a Communist in the cabinet.

There seems little reason, in view of these figures, to doubt that the Communist party today projects a new image. It has been reinforced by its accord with the Socialist party. The party belongs to the Left and it remains the "first party of the Left." But the Left has changed. Residual slogans and ideological pronouncements remain, but the Communist party is moving steadily in the direction of a parliamentary party. It is seeking votes, making alliances, and is ready to cooperate in a government coalition. The party is becoming a party like all others. It is the creature of a modernizing democratic society operating increasing under the restraints of an open political system in a manner consistent with its political tradition and culture. And, because its main supporters —the workers—are progressively assimilated in the system, the party is likely to become their spokesman and lobbyist *in* the system rather than to play the role of the vanguard of class struggle and revolution. It is likely to become more of a link and less of a spark. In fact, the identification of a sizable segment of the workers with the party may (as with the Labour party in Britain) be much more a sign that the party and the workers are being assimilated into a system than an indication of the revival of class warfare and revolutionary politics.

The party remains relatively young (but not appreciably more so than the Socialists or the Centrist party) and masculine. Its support from among the employed and middle cadres corresponds to the national percentages. Despite its loss of strength among the farmers, it has received 23 percent of the votes from those who live in rural communes and 19 percent of the "retired" and "inactive." What distinguishes the party, however, is that the majority of its voters come from the workers. Yet no more than 30 to 35 percent of *all* workers have been voting for it. It is naturally less strong among the managerial personnel, the liberal professionals, and small and large businessmen. The party has been consistently attempting to broaden its voting strength among all groups. The likelihood of its doing so has become even greater with the change in its ideological posture.

THE SOCIALIST PARTY

In the presidential election of 1969 the Socialist party reached its lowest electoral depths when its candidate barely managed to attain 5 percent of the vote. From then on the party went through many internal crises and divisions. Its factions could not agree on policies and leaders, nor could they settle the crucial question of their relationship with the Communist party. In 1971 the party came under the control of François Mitterrand, who was able to bring into it the young intellectuals who had played an important role in the formation of a broad non-Communist Federation of the Left. It was time, for the party electoral strength had been declining, its membership and regional leaderships were in shambles, and its finances were in a state of collapse.

The French political scientist Maurice Duverger spoke of the "radicalization" of the Socialists, who were increasingly a party of notables with regional strongholds and with middle and lower middle-class support. In joining hands with the Communists and reaffirming its commitment to limited nationalization, the Socialist party was again making a bid for the leftist vote. A small group of Radical-Socialists joined the Socialists, primarily for local electoral reasons. Together they reconstituted the *Union de la Gauche Démocrate et Socialiste* (UGDS) (Union of Democratic and Socialist Left). It showed new strength among many categories that had been abandoning it: workers, young people, white collar workers, and liberal, professional, and middle managerial groups. It, too, like the Communist party is attempting to broaden its appeal.

THE RÉFORMATEURS

"France is governed in the center" is a familiar slogan. But the Center consisted of remnants of various parties and groups of the Fourth Republic that were neither with the Gaullists nor with the Left. Some came from the MRP; some from the Radicals who refused to join the Socialists; some from Socialists who refused to ally with the Communists; some from the Independents and even from disenchanted Gaullists. A *Mouvement Réformateur* (Reform Movement), led by centrists who refused to join the "majority coalition," was established in 1972.

The *Réformateurs* are a party of notables, a party without organization and membership to speak of, and a party open to a number of minuscule groups. It is a party, finally, whose leadership was divided between the old leader of the Democratic Center and the new leader of the truncated—if not moribund—body of the Radical Socialists. The *Réformateurs* have lived a political life predicated upon an electoral strategy that is both simple and transparent: to win enough votes on the first ballot in as many constituencies as possible, and then to negotiate with the Gaullists the conditions under which they would throw their support behind them on the second ballot. Those conditions included a broadening of the government "majority" and of course a change in the composition of the government, to include some of their leaders.

THE GAULLISTS

While the Communists seemed to be undergoing significant transformations and the Socialists seemed to be gaining new support, while the centrist groups managed to avoid extinction by organizing what in effect was an electoral coalition, the Gaullists and their allies also seemed to be going through notable changes. "The Gaullist Phenomenon," as Jean Charlot has entitled his book describing the emergence and predominance of the Gaullist party, has been a part of French political history ever since the Liberation—and even before. Supporters of DeGaulle were attracted by his personality, his war record, and his commitment to French independence. They came from all social groups, cutting across the traditional class, party, and regional alignments. In 1951 the RPF *(Rassemblement du Peuple Français)*, the first party label given to the Gaullist movement, received 21.2 percent of the popular vote on the first ballot.

In May 1958 the Gaullist forces and General DeGaulle got a new —and, as it proved, quite a long—lease on life. The French Army fighting to stamp out Algerian independence stood up against the government of the Fourth Republic and called for the formation of a government of national unity. General DeGaulle and his followers seized the opportunity to return to power. The Parliament nominated DeGaulle as Prime Minister and gave him full authority to prepare a new Constitution and submit it for popular approval. When it was overwhelmingly approved, the UNR *(Union pour la Nouvelle République)*, the second Gaullist party label, won 20 percent of the vote in the legislative election of November 1958. The percentage for the Gaullist party, however, would have been much higher had it not been for the fact that *all* political parties, except the Communists, came out to support "the task of General DeGaulle." In 1962 the UNR–UDT *(Union Démocratique du Travail)*, the third party label, won 35.4 percent of the vote and a clear majority in the National Assembly; in 1967 the *Ve République* (the fourth party label) won 37.7 percent of the popular vote but barely managed a majority in the National Assembly because many centrists voted for the Communist-Socialist alliance on the second ballot. In 1968, however, the Gaullist-led coalition, running under their fifth party label, UDR *(Union de Démocrats pour la République)*, swept the election with 43.6 percent of the vote. In 1969, whatever doubts there might have been about the viability of the Gaullists without DeGaulle were put to rest by the victory of Georges Pompidou in the presidential election. Pompidou received 44 percent of the vote on the first ballot and 57 percent on the second. The legislative election of March 1973 gave the answer to those who continued to have lingering doubts about the political viability of the Gaullists as a party.

What has accounted for this extraordinary phenomenon? First, DeGaulle himself imparted a unifying thrust to the movement. He appealed strongly to all political families of France. A "catch-all" man was likely to impart a "catch-all" attitude into his movement. He had attacked the monied and business interests; he had restored the Republic when it was within his power to establish a personal government after the Liberation; he had associated Communists with his cabinet, and had introduced some of the most significant structural and social reforms, including economic planning. But he was also a devout Catholic, an army man, and a strong nationalist who believed in restoring political authority by strengthening the Executive and bolstering the authority of the State. But DeGaulle imparted to the movement also a sense of pragmatism. With the highest contempt for ideologies, he envisioned the future in terms of the real dimensions of our times: economic development, modernization, economic expansion and an intelligent and equitable distribution of the national product among various classes; that is, a commitment to a growing social and economic equality. This has been in essence the "program" of the Gaullists and their allies.

Electoral tactics reinforced the "catch-all" character of the Gaullists. They have shown themselves to be masters of coalition politics, absorbing or allying themselves not only with individual political leaders but also with political factions and groups. The Independents, the MRP, the Radicals, and in general the centrist "family" had been until 1973 both the victims and the beneficiaries of the Gaullist appetite. In joining the Gaullists, these groups committed themselves to the new institutions of the Republic and to the leadership of DeGaulle and his lieutenants and later of Pompidou. Only the Communists, the Socialists, and some centrists managed to resist. (See Table 3-3.)

The Gaullists increased and broadened their electoral support, developed an organization, broadened their membership to include about 200,000 members, and developed a leadership with power to provide discipline and to sanction deviations. They absorbed the various stragglers and brought under their label the various factions and groups from the Center. They became a national, well-organized coalition that overshadowed the rest. With its new and sixth party label—

TABLE 3-3: THE EVOLUTION OF THE "GAULLIST-COALITION" ELECTORATE

	1973	1968	1967	Adult pop.
		(Gaullists and Assorted Allies)*		
Sex				
Men	43%	46%	42%	48%
Women	57	54	58	52
	100	100	100	100
Age				
21–34	24		29	29
35–49	29		26	29
50–64	23		26	22
65+	24		19	20
	100		100	100
Occupation of Head of Household				
Top management, administration, business, liberal professions	7	6	5	6
Small business, merchant	9	14	11	9
Employed, middle echelon	19	18	16	17
Worker	21	25	28	32
Inactive	27	19	24	24
Farmer	17	18	16	12
	100	100	100	100
Residence				
Rural communes	38	40	34	30
Under 20,000 pop.	16	16	16	14
20–100,000	12	11	14	14
100,000 +	20	19	19	25
Parisian pop.	14	14	17	17
	100	100	100	100
Religion				
Practicing	28			
Occasionally	50			
Nonpracticing, Atheist	17			

*For every 100 voters.

Source: Roy Macridis, *The Modernization of French Politics.*

the URP (*Union des Républicains pour le Progrès*—Union of Republicans for Progress)—the Gaullists entered the 1973 election confident of remaining the dominant force within the dominant coalition.

If the Communists are no longer a revolutionary party, with all the symbolisms of the revolutionary Left with which they had been associated for so long, neither are the Gaullists a party of the Right with all the symbolisms associated with it for so long. Mainly, the Left and the Right have changed so much that the terms have become convenient landmarks with which only residual categories can be detected—matters of style and form, feeling and perception, whose weight when it comes to voting is declining.

The Legislative Election of 1973

What were the platforms of the political parties, and how sharply did they differ in 1973? What evidence do we have of the seriousness with which they were accepted by the electorate? On its face the election of 1973 appeared to be more related to programmatic declarations than did any previous election. The parties produced book-length programs dealing comprehensively with almost every aspect of society. No urgent international problems troubled the horizon. The election was mostly about the nature and goals of French society. On the surface this appeared to be a highly ideological election.

We shall discuss primarily the joint program of the Communists and the Socialists, that of the *Réformateurs* (the centrist oppositional group), and of course that of the Gaullists and their allies—the "majority." First, however, let us describe the parties that entered the electoral contest.

Little needs to be said about the party groupings of the extreme Right and the extreme Left, except that they shared the common predicament of intense infighting and fragmentation. On the extreme Right a number of groupings were unable to unite. Diehards for French Algeria, with the waning support of some of the refugees together with some of the old rightist groups hailing from the *Action Française,* managed to put together about 100 candidates. Their major purpose was to *influence* the "majority" and to prevent a victory of the Left. Similar disarray characterized the extreme Left. Trotskyite groups, fragments of the Fourth International, anarchists, and Maoists ran their individual candidates. All efforts to bring their forces together with the splinter Socialist faction, the PSU *(Parti Socialiste Unifié)* failed. The PSU, after surviving a number of internal splits, continued as a party of about 10,000 members. It had been able to capitalize on the leftist trend of the student uprising in 1968 and had managed to average just about 3 percent of the vote in the legislative elections held since 1958. It was the only serious formation left of the Communist party, consisting of genuine Socialist ideologues who constantly criticized both "the system" and the Communists.

The "big battalions" that were to confront each other were then four: the Communists, the Socialists, the *Réformateurs,* and the Gaullist coalition. The first two parties joined forces both politically and electorally. Politically they agreed on the same program—*Programme Commun de Gouvernement du Parti Communiste et du Parti Socialiste*—and they were referred to as *L'Union de la Gauche* (the Union of the Left). Electorally, they agreed to run independently of each other on the first ballot but vote for the candidate who came first on the second. The agreement was rigorously applied. There were no defections. One small qualification, however, should be made: while the Communists remained an individual, separate, centralized party, the Socialists ran together with some Radicals of the Left, under the party label of the *Union de la Gauche Démocrate et Socialiste.* The Communists and the UGDS ran candidates in virtually every constituency.

The *Réformateurs* represented old-time Radicals, various centrists, and even disgruntled Gaullists. Their leadership was shared by Jean Lecanuet, who had won 15 percent of the ballot in the presidential election of 1965, and Jean-Jacques Servan-Schreiber, a newcomer and progressive centrist who had managed to gain control of the old Radical party. He had produced the ambitious manifesto *Ciel et Terre* (Heaven and Earth), which was later modified and condensed into the *Projet Réformateur*—to become the platform of the centrists.

Both the UGDS and *Réformateurs* were coalition parties. But while the UGDS was under the control of the Socialists (they designated nine-tenths of the candidates for a total of 435, as opposed to 43 for the Radicals), the *Réformateurs* consisted of a number of groupings in which the old centrist groups under Lecanuet ran into constant competition and friction with the Radicals and others. The *Réformateurs* designated about 350 candidates.

The Gaullists and their allies formed a coalition consisting of three separate groups: the Gaullists (UDR), the Independent Republicans, and the centrists (the CDP—Center for Democracy and Progress). They all ran officially as the URP *(Union des Républicains pour Progrès).* They decided to join forces on the first ballot and designate one single candidate. This decision was not scrupulously adhered to. There were a total of 540 URP candidates: 359 from the UDR, 116 from the Independent Republicans, and 65 from the CDP, so that in a number of constituencies "majority" candidates confronted each other.

The central issues around which the election revolved were—as they almost always are—economic and social. But institutional problems as well as issues related to national defense and foreign policy were also prominent.

The Institutions

Institutional issues became prominent long before the election officially opened. What would happen if the Left won? More precisely, what would happen if the "majority" became a minority? Would the President dissolve the National Assembly and call for a new election, putting his office directly on the line? Would he ask the leader of the Left to form a cabinet? Did the elections revolve around the President and his policies and did they entail support or rejection of these policies? The prospect of an institutional crisis was constantly evoked by the parties of the Left.

The controversy about the Constitution and the stand taken by the various parties not only expressed a "legitimacy crisis" but also reflected the differences between Left and Right. The "majority" came out explicitly for presidentialism: for a "majority for the President," and for "support of the policy of the President." They considered the presidential election to be the most important national consultation. They adhered to the view that the basic policy directives and guidelines must come from the President, and that the legislative role of Parliament lies in deliberating and implementing them, that is, that its role is primarily supportive. As for the political role of the Assembly, the Gaullists seemed to exclude the notion that the President could ever appoint a Prime Minister of a different political persuasion. They indicated that if indeed the election were to bring forth a different majority, the President would have to pit himself against it by dissolving the National Assembly and calling for a new election. Hence, the broad construction of the Constitution and the notion that a parliamentary majority plays a supporting role remained the dominant outlook of the Gaullists. But they were willing to make qualifications: they favored a more open and free dialogue between Parliament and the Executive; they were willing to envisage a tighter parliamentary supervision of executive departments, the cabinet, and the Prime Minister; and they were in the process of conceding the need to shorten the President's term of office from seven to five years.

While accepting grudgingly the Gaullist constitution, the Socialist-Communist common program moved in the direction of parliamentarism. First, they insisted on proportional representation, a move calculated to undermine and perhaps to destroy the majority support that a President (any President) could ever have in the National Assembly. They also favored constitutional reform in order to do away with the abuses of personal power. They advocated the abolition of Article 16, which provides that in case the institutions of the Republic and the integrity of its territory are threatened in "a grave and immediate" manner, interrupting the regular functioning of the public authorities, the President of the Republic may take any measures required by the circumstances. They also urged that Article 11 be abrogated. This article allowed the President to submit to the people through a referendum not only constitutional changes but also major policy options. The President should not "appeal to the people over the heads of Parliament." Constitutional reforms should take place only through Article 89—that is, with the approval of the two legislative assemblies according to specific rules and requisite majorities. The Left also favored restoring parliamentarism through modification of the relevant articles of the Constitution in order to broaden the legislative role of the National Assembly.

The Center parties, while professing to avoid constitutional debates, moved cautiously in the direction of parliamentarism. They urged the introduction of an electoral system similar to that of the German Federal Republic, thus moving at least halfway in the direction of proportional representation. Similarly, in at least one of their statements the centrists excluded the hypothesis of a President's pitting his will and his office against a duly constituted parliamentary majority. They seemed inclined to put their emphasis upon Article 20, which gives the Prime Minister and the cabinet policy-making power, and considers the President more of an "arbiter" than a policy-maker.

In summary the basic position taken by the two most important political forces regarding the Constitution appeared to be what they had always been. Yet there were so many qualifications that the distance between the two was no longer as great as it had been in the past. The Left, with the support of some of the centrist leaders, favored "parliamentarism" rather than parliamentary supremacy. That is, the Left was anxious to see a number of prerogatives restored to Parliament without concentrating *all* powers in its hands. It went out of its way to accept some important aspects not only of presidentialism but also of executive leadership and government stability. For instance, the election of the President by direct universal suffrage was not questioned; nor was the power of dissolution to be set aside. The scope of legislative power of the National Assembly was to be extended, but there would be no wholesale return to legislative omnipotence. No return to the parliamentary committees of the Fourth Republic was envisaged, and the law-initiating predominance of the Executive was recognized.

As for the Gaullists, their desire to shorten the duration of the presidential mandate and their emphasis upon an increased dialogue between Parliament and the Executive and a greater legislative supervision corresponded to a shift away from the strict Gaullist presidential conception of the Constitution. The Gaullist party sought a better balance between President and Parliament through formal and informal consultative mechanisms. While the differences in overall direction and interpretation between Gaullists and the Left were clear, the sharp edges had been dulled.

Foreign Policy and Defense

Major differences among parties with regard to foreign policy and defense involved on the one hand the "Atlanticists with independence" (Gaullists) and those favoring "independence without Atlanticism" on the other (the Left, but particularly the Communists). The parties also disagreed on the extent and degree of "Europeanism" and the fate of the *force de frappe* (the French independent atomic and nuclear force). The Gaullists went all the way in support of the Gaullist foreign policy line: independence within the Atlantic alliance; European economic unity and expansion of the Common Market (but without any integrative common political institutions—at least not until a political union is laid down by 1980); insistence upon consultative decision-making processes in which the sovereignty of the individual states is safeguarded; the maintenance of the *force de frappe* as the best safeguard of French independence; a continuing effort to do away with two blocs (one dominated by the Soviet Union and the other by the United States) and an intimation that France ought to play a particularly important role in the Mediterranean and in the Middle East, where there was a possible confrontation between the two superpowers; and of course support to the United Nations resolution of 1967 regarding Israel. Minor differences within the majority groups could be noted, especially with regard to Israel and Europe; the CDP favored a more conciliatory attitude vis-a-vis the Israeli position, and both the CDP and the Independent Republicans were noticeably more "pro-European" than the Gaullists.

It was the *Réformateurs* who assumed a clearly pro-European stance; they favored integrative political arrangements and institutions and a popularly elected European parliament. A united Europe, they claimed, was the only instrument capable of resisting the American preponderance and the Soviet threat. The *Réformateurs* preached strict neutrality toward the Middle East; participation in the disarmament conference; and an end to France's role as the major salesman of arms in the world. They argued for reducing the French defense budget by 25 percent and for the development of a joint European nuclear deterrent.

The Left's position can be summarized as independence without the Atlantic alliance, without any European integrative alliance, and without the *force de frappe.* They emphasized global disarmament; the signing of nonaggression treaties with as many countries as possible (including, of course, the Soviet Union); the immediate abandonment of nuclear tests and an end to the fabrication of nuclear weapons, with the reconversion of atomic energy installations to domestic use; the cessation of sales of arms to any "racist" or "colonial" or "fascist" regimes. An immediate dissolution both of the Atlantic alliance and the Warsaw Pact was called for, but defensive alliances depending upon changing situations and needs were not to be excluded.

There were differences, however, between the Communists and the Socialists. For instance, the Socialists were unwilling to castigate American imperialism without being free to criticize Soviet policies; and their position in the Middle East appeared to be far more flexible with regard to the establishment of the Israeli frontiers than the 1967 United Nations Resolution, which the Communists accepted.

A sharp Left-Right dichotomy could not be discerned on foreign policy questions. The Communists were closer to the Gaullist position with regard to the Common Market, which they grudgingly accepted as a loose cooperative arrangement as long as it was not allowed to interfere with individual governments' attempts to solve national economic and social problems. While the Communists and the Gaullists differed on the need and duration of the Atlantic alliance, they seemed to agree on the overall dangers of American influence and control. There were some differences on some specific questions, such as the sale of arms and the *force de frappe.* But Communists and Gaullists again converged on their attitude vis-a-vis Israel. All in all, while it is easy to point to differences due in part to ideological positions (for example, sales of arms) or to the pro-Soviet stance of the French Communists (but not necessarily the Socialists) on the one hand, and the anti-Soviet posture of the French Right (but not necessarily of the Gaullists) on the other, divergences between Left and Right were not significant.

Economic and Social Issues

Two major ideological positions concerning social and economic policies can be distinguished: maintenance of the economic status quo by the "majority" and *Réformateurs;* and limited nationalizations by the Communists and Socialists. The main choice was between maintaining the basic structure of the economy as it developed under the Gaullists —indeed, ever since the Liberation—and structural reforms toward gradual nationalization. Otherwise, programmatic positions differed only in degree, with the Left proposing a little more of everything for everybody and a little less for the privileged few. But in some cases the

Gaullists promised the same, so that both sides argued with each other with the same slogans and brandished the same policy suggestions down to identical percentage figures.

The Gaullists constantly used the terms "expansion," and "progress," and "growth"; the Left used the slogans "advanced democracy," "equality," and "income redistribution." There was no question, even for the Communists, of ushering in socialism. Rather the emphasis was placed upon creating, or beginning to create, the *conditions* that would *ultimately* lead to socialism. While the Gaullists and the Center proposed no nationalizations, the Left proposed the immediate nationalizations of nine industrial "groupings" and state participation through purchase of stock in four others. In addition, insurance companies and most of the banks were to be nationalized, and state participation in many other economic activities—notably transport and telecommunications—was to be strengthened. Private owners were assured of an equitable compensation with special consideration for the small shareholders.

On most other economic issues, differences were incremental. The Left proposed to lower taxes for the "working population" and increase them for the private firms and corporations; to tax the higher income brackets; to eliminate the TVA (sales tax) for all necessities; to do away with fiscal exemptions for stockholders; to suppress all business deductions; to impose capital levies; and to eliminate depreciation allowances. To avoid the flight of capital that many claimed would be inevitable if the Left won, they planned to impose rigorous exchange controls and tight measures against the multinational corporations.

The Left then proceeded to outline in detail their social measures: 700,000 housing units a year; minimum monthly salary of 1,000 francs (about $200.00); increase in family allowances; retirement at 60 for men and 55 for women; gradual introduction of a completely free medical care system; reforms of social security by gradually reducing the contributions of salaried personnel; control of credit though the Bank of France and special credit allocations to small town and local units for developing social services and improving them. No longer did the Left attack the French economy for its inefficiency or low productivity, as it had done consistently as late as 1967. It even conceded that the real wages of the workers had improved! But the Left stressed the disparity of living conditions and incomes and argued in favor of a more equitable distribution of the national wealth. Its specific measures were aimed toward reaching a more egalitarian society as soon as possible by taxing the wealth, by imposing controls, and by simply distributing more in money and services to the less privileged.

The Gaullists did not stay on the defensive, but moved toward a pragmatic and comprehensive view that favored broad social and welfare legislation with a commitment to a more equal distribution of the national wealth. Nothing illustrates this better than their programmatic statement embodied in a speech (*Discours de Provins*) made by the Prime Minister. Never in the past had a reputedly rightist political party presented such a detailed bill of social and economic accomplishments and concrete social and welfare pledges. Gaullist accomplishments included a rate of economic growth of 6 percent for 1972 and an average annual rate of economic growth of 5 percent; the development of middle-sized towns (with a specific pledge to build swimming pools in every town with more than 10,000 people!); and priority in allocating resources for social services. There was more employment and opportunities in the provinces. The purchasing power of the less privileged had doubled between 1958 and 1972; and savings had increased by 70 percent for a corresponding period.

The Gaullists now promised to lower taxes on the lower income groups; provide equal pay for men and women; increase the pay of civil service to bring it into line with corresponding salaries in the private sector; and make additional efforts to "humanize" labor conditions. They pointed out with particular pride that in 1969 the paid annual vacation period was increased from three to four weeks. Two hundred nursery schools *(crèches)* were to be built. They promised six hundred thousand new housing units a year and special rental subsidies for older people were to be made available. All minimum old age pensions were to be raised; within five years, retirement was to be made possible at the age of sixty at rates paid for those retiring now at 65. The minimum monthly salary was to be raised to 1,000 francs—about $200. They promised to double the number of telephones available to households. Last but not least, they pledged to encourage the workers to seek increased participation in the profits of the firm where they worked. "We are the party of change!"; "We represent change; we represent movement"; "Never has France changed so much and so rapidly as in the last fifteen years," the Gaullist leader asserted in announcing the program.

While exceptions can be taken to many of the figures and doubts raised about many of the promises, this detailed account indicates the concreteness and specificity of the "majority" program and of its pronounced social, economic and welfare orientation. The vocabulary and the content of the program did not belong to the right-wing mentality. The Gaullists had moved far more forward (or leftward) and developed sophisticated arguments favoring planning, revenue sharing, and an income policy based upon a growing productivity of labor and reallocation of revenues. As a result they seemed to be saying that through their practices and economic mechanisms they were much more likely to bring about what the Left aspired to through outworn mechanisms and doctrinaire statements.

We must now ask how significant were the party platforms for the electorate. How clearly were they perceived by the people? Did platforms make a critical difference in the manner in which the electorate intended to vote? One public opinion survey provides us with a negative answer. Among those who intended to vote for the "majority," 21 percent said they were planning to do so because there was no alternative; 19 percent to show their loyalty to the ideas of General DeGaulle; 16 percent to show their confidence in Pompidou; 12 percent to show their confidence in the Prime Minister; and only 13 percent because they agreed with the platform of the "majority." (Nineteen percent did not respond.) For those intending to vote for the Left, 41 percent said they planned to do so because they were dissatisfied with the policies of the government; 10 percent because they had confidence in the leaders of the parties of the Left (Mitterrand and Marchais); 13 percent because they felt the Left had a chance to win; and only 14 percent because they agreed with the Common Program of the Left. (Twenty-two percent did not respond.) Similarly, after the Common Program had been agreed on, it did not seem to particularly excite the voters. In July 1972, 42 percent of all respondents declared that the Common Program, with a number of nationalizations advocated, was not a reason for them to vote either *for* or *against* a candidate of these two parties. Twenty-one percent had no opinion. Only 21 percent declared that the Common Program was likely to make them vote for the Left, and only 16 percent that it was likely to make them vote against the Left.

CAMPAIGN AND TACTICS

The formal "opening" of the campaign gave the candidates and parties several privileges: radio and television time on the state-controlled media (two hours to the "majority" and two hours to the opposition groups); reimbursement for certain campaign expenditures; the right to hold meetings in each electoral district at designated public places; and the right to print, post, and mail statements and posters describing the affiliation and position of each candidate.

The President of the Republic, after refusing to state his intentions in case the opposition groups won, and after indicating that the election was a contest between the Marxist-Socialists and "all others," refused to be drawn further into the campaign until the first balloting was over. The major party leaders campaigned actively and traveled and spoke all over the country in support of their respective candidates. But the meetings were not well attended, and appearances of candidates in their districts drew few voters.

The electoral tactics of the parties had been set before the campaign began, and the designation of candidates in the various districts

(473 for metropolitan France and 17 in the overseas territories and departments) had been prepared in advance. The URP–"majority" had decided to designate one single candidate for each constituency, but in about fifty districts there was a sort of "primary" among "majority" candidates for the second ballot. While this tactic preserved unity, it also limited the choice of the voters on the first ballot and may have accounted in part for the fall in the overall vote of the URP. To the Left exactly the opposite tactic was followed: almost all left-wing parties—extreme Left and PSU (510), Communists (476), and Socialists (471)—had candidates in virtually every constituency, spreading the net wider and catching more votes. Socialists and Communists agreed, however (and the extreme Left, though no party to the agreement, did the same), to vote on the second ballot for the one of their candidates who had come first. Extreme Left, Communists, and Socialists accounted between them for at least 1,400 candidates, as opposed to 540 for the "majority." The *Réformateurs* designated about 350 candidates with the hope of getting enough votes to stay on the second ballot in a number of constituencies and be in a position to negotiate with and influence the majority. All in all, together with the inevitable candidates of the extreme Right and the proliferation of candidates in a number of districts for local or personal reasons there were some 3,200 candidates for metropolitan France to contest 473 seats—on the average seven candidates for every district.

The electoral system is a modified version of the single-member district majority system, which was common during a great part of the Third Republic. The candidate who wins an absolute majority of the voters on the first ballot carries his district. If no candidate wins a majority, there is a runoff in which only candidates who received more than 10 percent of the registered votes are free to run again. The 10 percent "elimination clause" was introduced in 1966 with the overt purpose of eliminating small parties and individual candidates from the second ballot. Between the first and the second ballot, candidates who have the right to run can withdraw in favor of those who have a better chance. In a close political contest, therefore, the second ballot and how withdrawals will be made and voters will transfer their votes is more critical than the overall showing of the political parties on the first ballot. There are several variables: alliances and political affinities, the discipline of the voters in transferring their votes in accordance with the instructions of the candidate for whom they voted on the first ballot, and voter turnout. These variables all apply, as we shall see, with particular strength to the centrist vote, where weakness on the first ballot may be taken for granted but whose weight on the second becomes far more crucial than its numbers warrant.

Before we analyze the results of the 1973 election, two observations should be made. First, there was a higher level of participation than in any preceding legislative election. Almost 81 percent of registered voters went to the polls. Second, despite the proliferation of candidates, 90 percent of the votes went to candidates of the four major parties. Socialists, Communists, and the URP accounted for almost 80 percent. The second ballot reinforced this trend. The overwhelming majority of the votes—as much as 93 percent—went to the three major formations—Communists, Socialists, and Gaullists. The evidence showed clearly polarization and simplification of the party system.

THE RESULTS—FIRST BALLOT

The results of the March 1973 election were remarkably close to those of March 1967. (See Table 3-4.) The votes for the Communists, the PSU, and the centrist party—the *Réformateurs*—showed little change over the six-year period. The Communists slipped by about 1 percent, which the PSU and the extreme Left seemed to gain. The Socialists (UGDS) gained as much as 1.5 percent, despite the loss of some of the Radicals to the *Réformateurs*. Finally, the "majority" candidates—the Gaullists with their allies—lost from 1 percent to about 2 percent. Within each "coalition party," however, the shifts were more significant. Within the UGDS the Socialists received 19.19 percent of the votes and their radical allies only 1.51 percent. Within the URP, the Gaullists (UDR) received 23.93 percent, the Independent Republicans 6.83 percent, and the centrist splinter (CDP) 3.72 percent. For every three votes cast for the "majority," only two were given to the Gaullists. The overall trend between 1967 and 1973 was stability for all political formations, with a slight loss for the Gaullists and a slight gain for the Socialists. The Center survived. The *Réformateurs,* despite the loss of those who formed the CDP to join the Gaullists, maintained their strength.

When we compare the results of 1973 to those of 1967—the best year for the Left in the Fifth Republic—there is an overall swing from the "majority" to the opposition parties (mostly attributable to the Socialists) of about 1.5 percent. The combined Left received 46.3 percent of the total vote and the URP with its allies 38.5 percent.

Given the closeness of the voting strength of the major parties, the first ballot produced only few winners. Out of the 490 seats contested there were only 59 candidates who won with an absolute majority: 8 Communists, 1 Socialist, 27 UDR, 13 Independent Republicans, 6 CDP (for a total of 46 for the URP) and 5 independents "associated" with the "majority." The *Réformateurs,* with 12 percent of the vote, had little with which to console themselves. One hundred forty-five of their candi-

TABLE 3-4: FIRST BALLOT RESULTS IN 1967, 1968, AND 1973

	March 5, 1967	June 23, 1968	March 4, 1973
Registered	28,300,936	28,181,848	30,672,952
Abstentions	5,898,712 (19.07%)	5,649,441 (20.04%)	5,861,638 (19.11%)
Voting	22,902,224 (80.92%)	22,532,407 (79.95%)	24,811,314 (80.88%)
Null or void	512,710 (1.81%)	385,192 (1.36%)	552,264 (1.80%)
Votes-total	22,389,514 (79.11%)	22,147,215 (78.58%)	24,259,050 (79.08%)

VOTES

Parties	March 5, 1967	June 23, 1968	March 4, 1973
Communist Party	5,039,032 (22.51%)	4,434,832 (20.02%)	5,156,619 (21.26%)
PSU and Extreme Left	495,412 (2.21%)	873,581 (3.95%)	810,645 (3.34%)
Federation of the Left	4,224,110 (18.96%)	3,660,250 (16.53%)	4,939,603 (20.36%)
Various Leftists	319,651 (1.42%)	160,482 (0.74%)	314,604 (1.29%)
Democratic Center	2,829,998 (12.04%)	2,289,849 (10.34%)	3,015,472 (12.43%)
Fifth Republic (Gaullists)	8,448,982 (37.73%)	9,667,532 (43.65%)	8,364,904 (34.48%)
Various Moderates (pro-Gaullist)	621,097 (3.36%)	917,758 (4.14%)	972,623 (4.0%)
Extreme Right ⎫	191,232 (0.85%)	28,736 (0.13%)	684,580 (2.82%)
Various Rightists ⎭		111,125 (.50%)	

Source: Le Monde, March 6, 1973.

dates were eliminated for having failed to get the requisite 10 percent of the registered votes, but another 137 did better and were legally entitled to remain on the second ballot. An additional 25 did well enough to have a chance of being elected: 16 had placed first in their districts and 9 second. The Communists arrived first in 79 districts and the UGDS in 66. But the Socialists ran ahead of the Communists in about 140 constituencies. The Left candidates were represented on the second ballot in a total of 375 out of the seats to be contested.

Geography and Sociology of Voters

The overall distribution of URP-Opposition vote in 1973 was, however, reminiscent of the Right-Left voting patterns of the past. The Communist vote declined from 22.5 percent in 1967 to 21 percent, despite a decade of rapid industrialization, the influx of younger voters, and the death of DeGaulle (who always attracted workers' votes). The Communists maintained the strong positions they held in 1967 in the Paris suburbs and in the industrialized Northeast. They continued to show strength in the Marseille area and in some of the less developed regions. The Socialists made spectacular gains in many regions where they had been weak: notably in the West, East, and Southwest, and in Paris, where they improved by about 30 percent. They fell behind or barely managed to maintain their position in their traditional strongholds—Nord, Pas-de-Calais, and the Marseille area. In a number of areas, particularly in traditional Catholic ones, they cut into the Gaullist strength.

The URP remained strong. It received 40 percent of the vote in 38 departments and exceeded the absolute majority in four—Cantal, Haute Loire, Mayenne, and Vendee—considered among the most conservative. They slipped, however, in Paris and the Paris region, and in many working-class areas where Gaullism had attracted a number of votes. For instance, in 86 constituencies where the working-class population was high they received only 23 percent of the vote as opposed to 28.5 percent in 1967. And they also lost votes in the traditionally Catholic areas, East and West—some to the *Réformateurs* and some to the UGDS. Finally, the *Réformateurs* made some inroads into Gaullist votes. They managed between 20 and 25 percent of the vote only in a few departments, but maintained 10 to 15 percent in enough to make it possible for them to play a role on the second ballot.

The changes in the geography of the electorate were accompanied by noticeable shifts in the sociological composition of the electorate of major parties. Table 3-5 gives an overall composite profile of voters for 1973 *based upon their intention to vote.* The Gaullist electorate appeared older, more often feminine, and less urban, with less support from the workers and more from rural areas, the farmers, and the "inactive"

TABLE 3–5: PROFILE OF 1973 VOTERS BASED ON INTENTION TO VOTE (MARCH 1973)

	Communist Party	UGDS	PSU	Réformateurs	Gaullists	Various Rightists
For 100 voters in each category:	%	%	%	%	%	%
Overall	19	23	4	15	36	3
Men	22	25	4	16	30	3
Women	16	21	4	14	43	2
Age						
21–34	21	24	7	17	27	4
35–49	17	27	3	16	34	3
50–64	21	21	4	15	37	2
65+	17	18	1	10	52	2
Occupation of Head of Household						
Top management, administration, business	11	20	10	20	39	—
Small business, merchant	12	22	2	22	36	6
Employed, middle echelon	17	29	9	19	23	3
Worker	33	27	4	12	22	2
Inactive	17	20	3	14	44	2
Farmers	8	19	1	16	49	7
Residence						
Rural communes	13	21	2	14	46	4
Under 20,000 pop.	22	24	2	10	40	2
20–100,000	15	29	4	18	32	2
100,000+	21	24	5	15	32	3
Parisian pop.	28	18	8	19	25	2

Source: Roy Macridis, *The Moderization of French Politics: The Legislative Election of 1973*, p. 27.

population. The Communists, in contrast, appeared more masculine, more urban, and more than ever a workers' party, with a sharp decline among the farmers. Their overall support from rural areas and communes, however, showed only a small loss. The Communists also continued to receive appreciable support from the "inactive" groups of the population.

The electoral basis of the Socialist party showed more significant shifts. It improved its working-class support (with 27 percent of its votes coming from workers) and was only a little less masculine than the Communist party, but it was more youthful and stronger in small and average-size towns, with a fairly even support from among virtually all socioeconomic categories, especially among the salaried. But the *Réformateurs* also showed a relative change in their electoral base: in 1973 they received more votes from men than from women; more support from among the younger population groups; more support in the urban areas than in the rural communes. Twelve percent of their vote was from workers.

Internal Shifts

The overall stability of the vote, therefore, when compared with the 1967 results, hides internal shifts. Some shifts are numerical; others relate to regional and socioeconomic distribution of the electorate of the parties. The key in understanding numerical shifts is the vote for the *Réformateurs.* In 1967 the Democratic Center (which ran in opposition to the Gaullists) received 12.5 percent of the vote. In 1969 a faction— the CDP—led by two important centrist leaders joined the Gaullists, and in 1973 it ran with them. They received, as was noted, about 4 percent of the vote. Despite this, the *Réformateurs* (with some Radicals) received an almost identical percentage of the votes in 1973 that the Democratic Center received in 1967. On the other hand, the Gaullists and the Independent Republicans received about 38 percent of the vote in 1967, while the URP managed just 38.5 percent in 1973. The conclusion is inescapable: if we add the 4 percent of the votes brought to the URP by the centrist faction, the URP should have come out with at least 41 percent of the vote, instead of 38.5 percent. They lost about 3 percent, which must have shifted to the *Réformateurs* or elsewhere. Further, within the URP it was the Gaullists (UDR) that lost at least 6 percent (from 30 percent in 1967 to 24 percent in 1973). Alone they could not have maintained their position on the second ballot and won a majority of the seats in the National Assembly. The "majority" had become less Gaullist, with the centrist groups within it holding their own or gaining.

To the Left an analogous shift of votes occurred: the Socialist party balanced its forces with those of the Communists. Few new Socialist votes, however, came from the Communists. On the contrary, there is every indication that there was a transfer (almost equivalent to the one from the URP to the *Réformateurs*) from the *Réformateurs* and others to the Socialists. Something like 2 to 3 percent—representing not more than 500,000–700,000 voters—somehow shifted from the Gaullists to the *Réformateurs* and to the Socialists. Hence, despite their attachment to the Common Program, the Socialist party itself benefited on the first ballot from the centrist voters. The Left was no longer dominated by the

Communist party any more than the Right was by the Gaullists. The Center split its vote among the *Réformateurs* (12.5 percent), the Gaullists (about 10 percent), and the Socialists (about 3 percent). If we add these percentages we have a centrist vote of about 26 percent. The "centrist vocation" is ever present (see Table 3-6).

THE SECOND BALLOT

There is an old saying in France, according to which the voters choose their candidate on the first ballot and eliminate the others on the second. This adage has been restated by Jean Charlot with what purports to be mathematical precision, in what he calls "the law of the firsts." According to this "law," a candidate who places first on the first ballot has eight chances out of ten to win on the second; he who comes in second has two chances out of ten. The others have no chance. The "law" (but also the conventional wisdom of the saying) held in 1973. Yet, like all laws, it is based upon certain conditions, which have never been clearly stated. They depend on how the voters transfer their votes on the second ballot if their candidate either withdraws from the second ballot or is eliminated. While the URP came in first in twice as many electoral districts as the Communists and the Socialists together, there was no way of telling in advance what the voters would have done if the *Réformateurs* candidates who had gained more than 10 percent of the registered votes decided to stay on the second ballot. There were indications, to be sure, that if the election was close and if it pitted a Communist against a "majority" candidate, the *Réformateurs* would be inclined to abandon their candidate and vote for the "majority." But this was not so certain if the candidate who ran against a Gaullist was a Socialist. Further, what mattered more, conceding the propensity of the *Réformateurs* voters to move to "the majority," was an indication of the percentages that would go one way or another or into abstention. In 1967 some 35 to 45 percent of the centrists went Left or abstained, and this was almost enough to deprive the Gaullists of a majority in the National Assembly. To illustrate the crucial character of this shift we shall consider a hypothetical electoral district where the first ballot votes correspond by and large to the national averages.

Imaginary District—*La Belle France*
(Reg. voters: 50,000)

URP–Majority	17,000
Socialists	10,000
Communists	9,500
Réformateurs	6,500
PSU and Extreme Left	1,600
M. Dupont	
(Ind.-majority)	1,200

TABLE 3–6: POLARIZATION AND THE "CENTRIST VOCATION"

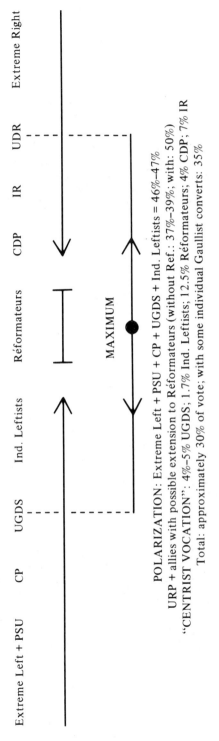

| Extreme Left + PSU | CP | UGDS | Ind. Leftists | Réformateurs | CDP | IR | UDR | Extreme Right |

POLARIZATION: Extreme Left + PSU + CP + UGDS + Ind. Leftists = 46%–47%
URP + allies with possible extension to Réformateurs (without Ref.: 37%–39%; with: 50%)
"CENTRIST VOCATION": 4%–5% UGDS; 1.7% Ind. Leftists; 12.5% Réformateurs; 4% CDP; 7% IR
Total: approximately 30% of vote; with some individual Gaullist converts: 35%

Source: Roy Macridis, *The Modernization of French Politics.* The essay was written and published before the presidential election. The total projected vote for the centrists corresponds very closely to the vote received by Giscard d'Estaing on the first ballot of the presidential election of May 1974.

If the *Réformateur* candidate stayed on for the second ballot, and if 50 percent of his voters voted again for him, then the Left would win even if four out of five of the remaining *Réformateur* votes went to the majority and one out of five abstained. The second ballot would look as follows: URP–Majority, 17,000, plus 2,600 (80 percent of half the *Réformateurs* votes), plus 1,200 (the Dupont votes) for a total of 20,800. The Socialist candidate would receive his own votes, plus the Communist's, plus the PSU's; the *Réformateur* candidate would receive 3,250 votes. The Socialist would win with a total of 21,100. This close victory would not be unusual, since about twenty-seven elections were decided by less than a 500–vote margin. In fact, the strategy of the URP leaders, after the first ballot, was precisely to avoid such triangular elections in which a *Réformateur* candidate might bring about a situation similar to our hypothetical case.

The crucial challenges for the "majority" before the second ballot therefore were to stem the Communist–Socialist wave, and to avoid triangular elections by inciting or cajoling the withdrawals of as many *Réformateurs* as possible from the constituencies where they could run. Last-minute indications of likely transfers (Table 3-7) made this imperative. imperative.

TABLE 3–7: TRANSFER OF VOTES FROM FIRST TO SECOND
BALLOT

Communist vs. "Majority" Candidates

	Communist Party	Majority	Undecided
Those Who Voted for *Réformateurs*	6	67	27
Those Who Voted Socialist	68	16	16

Socialist vs. "Majority" Candidates

	Socialist	Majority	Undecided
Those Who Voted for *Réformateurs*	17	64	19
Those Who Voted Communist	92	4	4

Source: In Roy Macridis, *The Modernization of French Politics*, p. 30.

Intensive trade-offs followed between the *Réformateurs*, who continued to profess their opposition to the URP, and the URP leaders. Within five days the *Réformateurs* "fell on their right side." They withdrew their candidates in more than 100 of the constituencies where they could legally run, in favor of the "majority" candidate—or, rather, against the Communist–Socialist alliance. In return the URP withdrew its own candidates in some twenty constituencies in favor of a *Réformateur*.

There were 360 straight contests. The Communists alone confronted 146 candidates of the URP, 16 *Réformateurs*, and seven moderate candidates who supported the majority; 148 Socialists confronted 145 URP and eight *Réformateurs*. There were only 64 triangular elections, involving in the majority of cases either a Socialist or Communist, a *Réformateur*, and a URP candidate. But in many of those the *Réformateur* vote could not affect the outcome.

As expected, the major beneficiaries of the second ballot were the "majority" candidates, who gained almost 2 million votes; the vote of the *Réformateurs* fell, despite the support some of their candidates received from the Gaullist voters, by almost 1.5 million. The URP gained about 10 percent on the second ballot; the *Réformateurs* lost 9.28 percent; and the Left dropped almost 1 percent. Transfers ran according to the predictions. But, while the Communist vote went overwhelmingly to a Socialist candidate (except in rare cases where the Socialist candidate had an anti-Communist record), in the regions where Communist–Socialist hostility has been traditional and endemic, the Socialist voters failed to reciprocate. Take, for instance, the 17th electoral district of Nord. The figures on the first and second ballot tell the story clearly:

	1st Ballot	2nd Ballot
Communist Party	11,630	18,477
UGDS (Socialist)	9,784	
URP	16,638	21,123 (elected)
Others	3,008	

Similar instances can be found in the Northwest in general and in the Marseille area in particular. Socialists abstained or even voted for the "majority," and in case of triangular elections Socialists transferred part of their vote to a *Réformateur*. The transfers finally showed the progressive polarization of the political parties: Communists, Socialists, and the URP received about 93 percent of the votes cast.

The "majority" remained the majority. The transfer of the *Réformateurs* and the defection of the Socialists helped them win a number of close contests. In contrast to 1967, the URP–"majority" came out safely with a comfortable parliamentary majority of 261 (or, if we add some 15 individual candidates who professed their attachment to the "majority" and were supported by it, 276) out of 490 seats. But the Gaullists (UDR) *alone* with 185 seats no longer controlled a majority, as they did in the 1968 Assembly. They were the "majority of the majority." Without their converts and allies they could not govern (Table 3-8).

The Communists and Socialists lost ground in the National Assembly in comparison to 1967, though they had a higher percentage of the popular vote. Their alliance generally worked well. The defection of the centrists—a defection that could not have been averted or neutralized—accounted for their defeat. The Left had received as many votes as it could ever hope to receive on the first ballot, and it could not improve its score. Had it received at least 40 percent of the centrist vote, or had the *Réformateurs* kept at least 50 percent of their followers behind their candidates on the second ballot, if they had decided to run again, the Left would have won the election. As it was, they elected 176 deputies in all, about twenty less than in their best year in the Fifth Republic, 1967.

TABLE 3–8: THE FRENCH NATIONAL ASSEMBLY,[1] 1967, 1968, 1973

	March 1967	June 1968[2]	March 1973
"Majority"			
UDR (Gaullists)	201	273	185
Independent Republicans	44	61	55
CDP (Centrist, Center for Democracy and Progress)[4]	–	–	30
Opposition			
CDP[4]	41	32	–
Reformateurs	–	–	34
Radicals ⎱ UGDS	101	53	100
Socialists ⎰			
Communists	73	34	73
Miscellaneous	7	30	13[3]

[1] The absolute majority in this 490-seat Assembly = 246 seats.
[2] February 1973 distribution; changes since 1968 due to party switches.
[3] Among these, *three* are from the extreme Left; *at least six* others are from the "majority."
[4] Joined "the majority" after 1969.

Source: Adapted from *Le Monde*, March 13, 1973.

The strategy of the *Réformateurs* to arbitrate between Left and Right and ultimately to use their weight to refashion the composition of the government backfired. Their predicament was an impossible one. Had they kept up their opposition to the URP by maintaining their candidates on the second ballot, they would have risked not only annihilation in the runoffs but also a Communist–Socialist majority. They had to settle for the only available course: an electoral agreement with the "majority" that salvaged them thirty seats in the National Assembly.

The composition of the new Parliament reflected to a limited extent the decline of the old traditional elites. One hundred fifty-five new members were elected, but out of those fewer than 110 entered Parliament for the first time, representing a renewal rate of the Assembly of less than 25 percent. Among the 490 deputies there were 69 educators from high schools and universities; 54 civil servants; 52 "managers"; 39 judges or lawyers; 39 doctors and surgeons; 21 company executives; 22 workers; 22 without a profession; 16 engineers; 15 judges of administrative tribunals; 15 newspapermen and writers; 14 salaried personnel; 13 merchants and salesmen; 11 from the foreign service; 6 veterinarians; 10 public notaries; 5 career politicians; and a scattering of others. The major shift from the past was the increase in the number of executive and managerial personnel and civil servants, as opposed to the decline in lawyers, farmers, public notaries, veterinarians, and so on. It is not as yet much of a shift, and the composition of the new Assembly does not yet reflect fully the new leadership group. But it is a move in this direction.

CONCLUSION

What was the electoral significance of the legislative election? What conclusions can be drawn from it regarding Left-Center-Right voting patterns and attitudes? Finally, what can be gleaned with regard to broader systemic trends?

From an electoral standpoint our overall conclusions are quite obvious. The 1973 election demonstrated stability; a slight increase of the Socialist vote; the ability of the "majority" to resist; the tenacity of the centrist vote but also its propensity to vote for the Gaullists on the second ballot; and a continuing gradual reduction of the Communist vote. The internal shifts, however, and some alteration in electoral geography indicate some new trends and directions. The most significant may be the relative "nationalization" of the major political parties, in the sense of a more even geographic distribution of their vote. This is particularly so with the relative penetration of the Socialists in forbidden Catholic territory but also "majority" gains in some of the old strongholds of the Left.

Socialists, Communists, and the URP seemed to stretch to every corner of the country and to as many socioeconomic categories as possible—they became national and aggregative. Yet, from a socioeconomic point of view, the division between the Left and the URP appeared to be pronounced. The workers clustered significantly behind the Communists and the Socialists. About 60 percent voted for the Left, as opposed to 49 percent in 1967. In contrast, only 21 percent of the workers voted for the URP, as compared to 28 percent in 1967. Catholics, despite some defections, continued to vote for the "majority"; more of the young people voted for the Left, which remained more urban and masculine. The opposite was true for the URP. These figures have led two extremely knowledgeable analysts to see the resurrection of the traditional Left-Right cleavage. For instance, Jean Charlot writes, "Whether we are talking about the sociology of the electorate, the tactics of the parties, or the transfers from the first to the second ballot—everything fits: the old Left-Right distinction that shaped political action in the Third Republic is back and has in effect replaced the Gaullist–anti-Gaullist division."[6] Alain Lancelot comments on the composition of the URP voters: "The staying power of the 'majority' hides a profound restructuring that may well do away with the originality of Gaullism—a movement cutting across all classes—in favor of the traditional sociology of the conservative electoral forces."[7]

There is a great deal to support Charlot's and Lancelot's contentions. The overall ideological thrust of the Left was unmistakable, though (as argued previously), differences in specifics—other than nationalizations—were incremental. There was a comprehensive ideological posture favoring equality, declaring war upon the commanding heights of the economic power of the top French bourgeoisie, and searching for new qualitative standards, for a new way of life. The alignment of the working class behind the *Union de la Gauche* gave to the election a class character that, as noted, was not so clear in the preceding legislative or presidential elections. The traditional "mystique" of the Left (it dies hard in France!) played a role, though again the enthusiasm, the commitment, the sense that it was a contest between "everything" and "nothing," and hence even the awareness on the part of the voters that this was an important ideological confrontation, were missing. Are we then confronted with a return to traditional ideological and class alignments, and do they signify a return to the ideological politics of the past? Is the legislative election of 1973 conclusive? I do not think so.

The Gaullist coalition cannot, as was indicated previously, be situated and identified with the traditional French Right, even if its geographic and socioeconomic base resembles the Right more than in any previous election. The French Right has moved a long way from its fixed positions since 1958. It approaches in its platform and overall policy recommendations an enlightened and moderate center favoring a welfare state. It projects a vastly different image from the traditional Right of the past, but the same is true of the Left. The two "families" have moved closer. There is a greater degree of sharing than ever before with regard to both political institutions and social values. Charlot admits this when he writes "the division between the two trends does not imply at all an explosive situation close to civil war."[8] In fact, notwithstanding the ideological postures of the two formations in their extreme poles, the opposite is true.

First—and this is a new phenomenon—the two formations were not running on the basis of sectarian and exclusive goals, as had been the case for the many parties that represented the Left and the Right in the past. They were running to get a majority to form a government. This "majoritarian vocation"—heretofore limited to the Gaullist coalition—is now shared by the Communists and the Socialists alike. Second, in so doing, the Left seems to have accepted fully the rules of the political game, promising the public to safeguard their future choice for another government whatever the popular verdict may have been in 1973. Third, both of the large formations were in fact "coalitions"—and coalitional politics involve a greater degree of compromise, a greater effort both to integrate and to aggregate the constituent units and the voters than ideological parties and politics. Finally, as I have argued, unless we consider "nationalizations" the keystone to the Left-Right division, the options given to the electorate by the two formations were not mutually exclusive. If we continue to maintain the labels Left and Right, we must admit that their respective approaches to the system and to the society, as well as their tactics, have changed. Though the labels may continue to be used, and though the landscape continues to be familiar, new wine has been poured into the bottles and new vineyards (to add an appropriate twist to the metaphor) have been planted.

Both of the two major formations tried to mobilize as much of the electorate as possible; both cast their net as wide as possible to attract various groups, marginals, drifters, and floaters; both sought to win a majority according to the best rules of a parliamentary game. The URP represented a broad centrist formation. This "centrist vocation" is in tune not only with overall societal development but also with the attitudes of the *new* working class. The middle class of today has undergone significant transformation, and the Center has as a result changed its aspirations and mentality. Nor are the workers still nurtured in the revolutionary tradition of the past. Both are the creatures of an unprecedented economic expansion and of a new and more progressive and open society. It is this new middle class that believes in institutional reforms, that performed so well under economic planning, that abandoned its protectionism and restructured its family-owned firms, that has spawned new socioeconomic groups: engineers, technicians, public servants, new universities, new agricultural cadres, and new cooperatives, that developed nuclear technology, that is in fact the political center of gravity. It is a new bourgeoisie that spans the ranks of the electorate from some of the Communists and many of the Socialists to the Gaullists. It is the real majority. Whether the Gaullist party as such disappears or not, whether a new Center coalition is formed, whether the Gaullists continue to assimilate other groups of the Center and even of the Left under various new electoral labels, the Center emerged as the real political force. This conclusion will be reinforced with the presidential election that followed a year later and to which we shall now turn.

ENDNOTES

1. For a detailed account of the election of 1973, see Roy Macridis, *The Modernization of French Politics: The Legislative Election of 1973* (University Programs Modular Studies, General Learning Press, 1974). A part of the material in this chapter is reproduced from it. Also, Jack Hayward and Vincent Wright, "Presidential Supremacy and the French General Election of March 1973," in *Parliamentary Affairs,* Summer and Autumn, 1973.

2. Stanley Hoffmann, ed., *In Search of France* (Cambridge, Mass.: Harvard University Press, 1963), pp. 1–117.

3. Beer and Ulam, eds., *Patterns of Government,* 3d ed. (New York: Random House, 1972), p. 88.

4. *Les Familles Politiques Aujourd'hui en France* (Paris: Editions de Minuit, 1966).

5. The figures are taken from Jean Stoetzel: "Le Vote à Gauche: Qui?" in Jean Charlot's *Quand la Gauche Peut Gagner* (Alain Moreau, 1973), pp. 11–20.

6. Charlot, *Quand la Gauche Peut Gagner,* p. 216.

7. Alain Lancelot, in *Projet* (June 1973), p. 680.

8. Charlot, p. 216.

chapter four

The Presidential Election, May 5–19, 1974

The sudden death of President Pompidou on April 2, 1974, ushered in a new feverish period of electioneering for the highest office in the land. The energy crisis, the controversy over relations between Europe and the United States, the war in the Mideast, the looming trade deficit and rapid inflation, the subsequent "floating of the franc" had created a state of emergency. The new majority or, for that matter, the "opposition" in the National Assembly were given no opportunity to debate the issues that were so prominent in the election. It had been a year of crisis and the Gaullist system was to be tested once more—perhaps definitively.

It was the first presidential election after DeGaulle's death with no heir apparent visible. Pompidou had been promised a "national destiny" by DeGaulle when he was politely but firmly removed from the office of Prime Minister in June 1968. Pompidou had been a firm and loyal associate of DeGaulle; a Prime Minister for six years; a skillful manager of election strategy (in 1967 and 1968) and a tough manipulator of the party organization while occupying the office of Prime Minister. He stood alone among the Gaullists to succeed the aging President. His only drawback was that he was not one of the "ancient Gaullists." But he had remained close to the leader and twenty-five years of personal and political service gave him a prominence that was grudgingly accepted by virtually all among the Gaullists. When DeGaulle resigned, therefore, there was no battle of succession. Pompidou announced his candidacy right away and the Gaullist party closed ranks behind him. DeGaulle himself kept a vigilant and approving eye but didn't speak a word in public. The Left was at the time sharply divided and was eliminated from the second ballot, which became a contest between a centrist, Alain Poher, and Pompidou. With the Communists counseling abstention on the second ballot, Pompidou's victory became a foregone conclusion. The results for the first and the second ballot are shown in Table 4-1.

TABLE 4-1: THE PRESIDENTIAL ELECTION, 1969

	First Ballot June 1		First Ballot June 1	Second Ballot June 15		Second Ballot June 15
		Percentage of Vote	Percentage of Voters Registered		Percentage of Vote	Percentage of Voters Registered
Registered	28,775,876			28,747,988		
Voting	22,500,644			19,851,728		
Abstaining	6,275,232 (21.80%)			8,896,260 (30.94%)		
Invalid	289,922 (1%)			1,294,629 (4.50%)		
Votes ent.	22,210,722 (77.18%)			18,557,099 (64.55%)		
	Votes	Percentage of Vote	Percentage of Voters Registered	Votes	Percentage of Vote	Percentage of Voters Registered
Pompidou (Gaullist)	9,763,428	43.95%	33.92%	10,686,498	57.58%	37.17%
Poher (Centrist)	5,202,271	23.42	18.07	7,870,601	42.41	27.37
Duclos (Communist)	4,781,838	21.52	16.61	—	—	—
Defferre (Socialist)	1,128,049	5.07	3.92	—	—	—
Rocard (PSUL)	814,053	3.66	2.82	—	—	—
Ducatel (No party)	284,820	1.28	0.98	—	—	—
Krivine (Extreme Left)	236,263	1.06	0.82	—	—	—

Source: Macridis and Ward, *Modern Political Systems, Europe,* 3rd ed., p. 251.

The new presidential election of 1974 was another matter. De-Gaulle was rapidly becoming a legend. Succession to the Gaullist leadership was no longer clear; nor had it been evident that Pompidou favored anybody in particular. Had he been given some time, he might have annointed his successor. Not only was he not given the time but some of the Gaullist leaders had moved in their party congress at Nantes in November 1973 against the President. Pompidou's men were elbowed out while the "orthodox" Gaullists moved on the scene behind Chaban-Delmas, who had been Prime Minister between 1969 and 1972.

What were the major questions that the forthcoming election for a new President were to answer? First and foremost was the ability of the political parties to designate their candidate. The matter proved to be crucial and may continue to be so. No matter how disorganized and fragmented the American parties are, they manage to perform one major function—to nominate a man as a candidate to the presidency. Would the French parties manage to do the same? Secondly, would the parties of the Left be able to live up to the exemplary record they had set in the legislative election by throwing their full weight behind one candidate on the second ballot—and perhaps, even better, by agreeing on a candidate from the start? In the presidential election of 1969 they were, as we noted, in disarray. Would their good showing in the legislative election provide for the desired unity and possibly for victory? And what about the political forces in the country? Would the Common Program be the binding platform of the "candidate of the Left" again? Was the division between the Left and Right that we noted to repeat itself? But on what substantive terms and issues? And what about the Center? Would it be crushed between the two or, as we hinted, revive at the expense of either the Left or the Right or at the expense of both? Would "presidentialism" be fully legitimized with the acceptance of the institutions of the Fifth Republic (an important part of the Gaullist legacy) or would there be a renewed bickering about the institutions? And above all, would the election present clear ideological options between the two candidates rather than convergence on policy declarations and specific electoral pledges?

The Electoral System

Before we answer these questions, a few words are needed about the French electoral system for the presidency. To begin with, anybody can become a candidate. The only requirement is a deposit of $2,000 that the candidate loses if he receives less than 5 percent of the vote and a "nomination" signed by 100 notables—deputies, senators, mayors, departmental counsellors. Since every candidate is given time on the national TV and radio networks (two hours) there is a temptation for many people to run. Even if they have no chance and are likely to forfeit their deposit, they have an opportunity to publicize at relatively low cost certain views or certain interests. The candidates who get more than 5 percent of the total vote get their deposit back plus an amount equivalent to about $20,000 for their expenses. They also have their electoral manifestos and some other related electoral expenses covered by the state.

To win on the first ballot a candidate must receive an absolute majority of the votes. This has never happened; even DeGaulle received less than 44 percent on the first ballot of the first presidential election of 1965. The second ballot is limited to *only two* candidates—those who came first and second (though the prospect of a withdrawal of one of them in favor of a third or fourth placed candidate is not excluded by the letter of the Constitution). The second ballot takes place two weeks after the first and the two protagonists are again given equal radio and TV time (about four hours each) to redefine their position and advocate their respective programs.

Thus, there are obvious similarities as well as differences between the electoral system for the legislative election and the presidential election. The saying we discussed "on the first ballot one chooses; on the second the voters eliminate" does not apply with the same force. Genuine choice, after the elimination of many candidates on the first ballot, takes place on the second one—where the contest is between two men. In 1965 and in 1969, DeGaulle and Pompidou came first and won on the second ballot but this did not prove to be the case in 1974. The practice of *ralliement* (of rallying to the support of one or the other of the two remaining candidates) by the defeated ones applies just as much in the presidential election as it does in the legislative ones. But whereas in the legislative elections triangular election may blur the issues, in the presidential election the defeated candidates, the parties, and the voters are forced to take sides. The presidential election is a strictly bipolar affair. It polarizes the electorate into what becomes a highly competitive electoral contest. The only way to blur it is massive abstention under the directives of a powerful political party as in 1969 when the Communists urged abstention from the second ballot. It is also a strictly majoritarian election. The candidate who gets elected gets an absolute majority (which is not necessarily the case with American presidential elections).

Given the ease with which candidates are nominated, but for many other reasons as well, the personal factor plays a more important role in designating candidates than the political parties. In 1965 a man virtually without a party, François Mitterrand, announced his candidacy to gain the support of the Socialists, some centrists and the Communists. As for DeGaulle, he announced his candidacy on his own without any consultations and without any reference to the Gaullist party that supported him. The same happened in 1969. There was no meeting of the Gaullist party to designate Pompidou—he simply proclaimed his candidacy and the Gaullists fell into line. The parties have not as yet played the role in designating the candidate that correlates in the long run with support, responsibility and voter mobilization. While the electoral system for the presidency is supposed to polarize choice, the manner in which the candidates are designated does very little to strengthen party structures and organization and to promote party leadership.

The Candidates

This lack of party strength became manifestly clear in the days following Pompidou's death for two reasons. First, there was a plethora of candidates (twelve in all) most of them self-designated. (See Table 4–2.) Second, with the exception of the Left—that is, the Communists, Socialists and left-wing radicals who deliberated before deciding formally to support a candidate (it was again François Mitterrand)—there was total disarray within and among all other formations. The groups to the left of the Communists—Trotskyites, Maoists, and other revolutionaries—failed to agree. Two candidates vied with each other, Arlette Laguiller and Alain Krivine, while some minuscule groups counselled abstention. The PSU remained eternally divided but it was decided finally not to designate its own candidate but to support the "candidate of the Left"—Mitterrand. The Center showed some discipline, but some of its leaders ran on their own. The *Réformateurs* divided and hesitated for a long time before deciding.

It was within the "majority" that the disarray was the most pronounced. The Gaullists and their allies split in their constituent parts which in turn split internally. At least three candidates emerged: Chaban-Delmas, the choice of the orthodox Gaullists, proclaimed himself a candidate even before the last funeral peroration on Pompidou had been spoken; Jean Royer, closely associated with the Gaullists and a member of the cabinet, was a champion of the small merchants, artisans and shopkeepers; and Giscard d'Estaing, Minister of Finance from 1962 to 1966 and 1969 to 1974. As the leader of the Independent Republicans he had joined the "majority." His party won 55 seats in the National

TABLE 4–2: THE PRESIDENTIAL ELECTION OF MAY 1974

FIRST BALLOT (May 5, 1974)

Total No.		Candidate	No. of Votes	%
Reg. Voters	30,602,953	François Mitterrand	11,044,373	43.24
Abstentions	4,827,210	(Leftist Coalition)		
Voters	25,775,743	Valéry Giscard d'Estaing	8,326,774	32.60
Blanks	237,102	(Ind. Rep. Party)		
		Jacques Chaban-Delmas	3,857,728	15.10
Valid Ballots	25,538,636	(UDR-Gaullist)		
		Jean Royer	810,540	3.17
% Total		(Minister in Gaullist Cabinet)		
Abstentions	15.08	Arlette Laguiller	595,247	2.33
Voters	84.91	(Workers' Struggle—		
Blanks	.76	Trotskyite)		
Valid Ballots	84.14	René Dumont	337,800	1.32
		(Environmentalist)		
		Jean-Marie Le Pen	190,921	.74
		(National Front)		
		Emile Muller	176,279	.69
		(Socialist Democratic Movement of France)		
		Alain Krivine	93,990	.36
		(Revolutionary Communist Front - Trotskyite)		
		Bertrand Renouvin	43,722	.17
		(New French Action (Action Française)— Monarchist)		
		Jean Claude Sebag	42,007	.16
		(European Federalist Movement)		
		Guy Heraud	19,255	.07
		(European Federalist)		

SECOND BALLOT (May 19, 1974)

Reg. Voters	30,600,775	Valéry Giscard d'Estaing	13,398,412	50.80
Abstentions	3,876,180			
Voters	26,724,595	François Mitterrand	12,975,625	49.20
Blanks	356,788			
Valid Ballots	26,367,807			

% Total

Abstentions	12.66
Voters	87.33
Blanks	1.16
Valid Ballots	86.16

Assembly in 1973. It is a "party of notables"—municipal, regional, departmental political leaders with no membership to speak of and little discipline and structure, and no carefully spelled out program. Did Giscard d'Estaing belong to the Gaullists or to the Center? Was his candidacy calculated to split the "dominant party" and to resurrect the centrist strength in line with the centrist vocation we discussed earlier? The fact that one of the leaders of the *Réformateurs*—Jean Lecanuet— immediately gave him his support gave reason to believe that this might be the case. Similarly, the other leader of the centrists—Jean-Jacques Servan-Schreiber—decided, after a long silence, to support him. The "other half" of the centrists, those that had been part of the "majority " (the CDP) came out strongly behind the Gaullist candidate—Chaban-Delmas.

Thus the "majority" of 1973 broke up. The Gaullist party was unable, notwithstanding all efforts made by the Prime Minister, to agree on a single candidate. Indeed with the President dead the Prime Minister was clearly shown to lack any force. The "President's man" had no influence when the President died! A number of Gaullist party leaders —notably among the parliamentarians and even some Ministers— equivocated. Some sided openly with Giscard d'Estaing; others refused to endorse Chaban-Delmas and still others gave only token assent. A "group of 43" was formed and pledged to support Giscard d'Estaing if he received more votes on the first ballot; the movement grew to 61 and perhaps to more. Among them were the Minister of the Interior and one of the Junior Ministers. The Prime Minister himself, whose aspirations to become the candidate of the "majority" were rebuffed, kept silent until the first ballot "out of loyalty to the party," only to throw his support behind Giscard d'Estaing as soon as the results of the first ballot became known. Only the central committee of the party, under a veteran political leader—Alexander Sanguinetti—held firm. But neither he nor the committee in its collective capacity could countenance the indifference of a Prime Minister, the hostility of the Minister of the Interior and of many parliamentarians, and fill the vacuum created by the silence of the only voice that could be listened to—the President's. The Gaullists had divided; the fight among the Epigones had broken out into the open. It is likely to spread and to fester.

While attention was focused on the predicament of the Gaullists, the other nominations were left unnoticed. Jean LePen ran for the extreme Right; even more to his right was Renouvin, a Monarchist; a professor, René Dumont, ran as an environmentalist; the Mayor of Mulhouse—a European Federalist and a centrist—threw in his hat. There were three more minor candidates, who received less than half a percent of the total vote on the first ballot.

The Campaign

The campaign was officially opened on April 19. All candidates but the spokesman of the "united Left," Mitterrand, the Gaullist, Chaban-Delmas, and the leader of the Independent Republicans, Valéry Giscard d'Estaing, seemed doomed to utter failure. It was originally thought that Jean Royer would take votes away from the Gaullist candidate and perhaps put Chaban-Delmas behind Giscard d'Estaing. Soon, however, when Royer came out forcefully against contraception and abortion by extolling the virile virtues of self-discipline, he became no threat to anybody.

Thereafter the campaign was dominated by two major considerations. The first was the credibility of François Mitterrand as the candidate of the Left and the extent of support he could rely upon. The credibility proved high and the support more extensive than anticipated. The Communist party, the left-wing Radicals, the Socialist party (of which he is the leader), and the PSU which had equivocated in the past, all considered him as *their* candidate. The Common Program fashioned before the legislative elections became the program of Mitterrand. The major trade union organizations: the Communist-controlled CGT (General Confederation of Labor); the Socialist CGT-FO (*Force Ouvrière*); the leftist CFDT (French Confederation of Democratic Labor); and, finally, the Federation of National Education (FEN) all came out for him. As the campaign progressed, the Extreme Left, speaking through Laguiller and Krivine, promised to throw their support behind Mitterrand, too, on the second ballot. The "Union of the Left" or *Union Populaire* (Popular Union) as it came to be called presented an unparalleled unity that had a powerful mobilizing effect upon the voters. The combined strength of the Left in the legislative election of March 1973 was almost 47 percent. With the sharp divisions in the Gaullist movement and nobody with DeGaulle's or Pompidou's stature to lead it, it was difficult to see how the Left could lose.

In the campaign before the first ballot, Mitterrand serenely argued for the Common Program, a new Socialist society, a new way of life, with drastic economic measures to bring inflation under control and ultimately to equalize opportunities and benefits and restructure and reform the capitalistic society. The Communists maintained their positions—the Common Program was a first and indispensable step in building Socialism—the establishment of "advanced democracy." But they were willing to qualify their position by stating that although the broad lines of the Common Program were binding on all, the presidential candidate was free to define his own presidential options. The Communists expected, in case of victory, to join the cabinet by receiving five to seven ministerial posts. The more extreme left-wing groups, sensing that this was perhaps the first real chance for the Left, softened their claims for specific reforms and argued that a government of the Left would be a better and more hospitable instrument for the realization of their ultimate revolutionary aims than a government of "the Right." In the opinion polls Mitterrand steadily progressed. Few predicted an outright victory but many hoped that a vote of 45–46 percent would make his position impregnable in the second ballot.

The second consideration seemed to support these hopes of the Left, but also to provide for a small dark cloud that later was to cause anxiety and ultimately defeat. For strangely enough, it may well have been the quarrels among the Gaullists which, by discrediting them, provided the opening that Giscard d'Estaing needed. The Gaullist leader fell into the trap that proved to be his undoing and the making of Giscard d'Estaing. He launched repeated attacks against his erstwhile associate. Chaban-Delmas, to the surprise of all, claimed to belong to the Center, while Giscard d'Estaing, a member of the "upper bourgeoisie" with aristocratic connections, was the man "of the Right." Yet opinion polls had shown that Giscard d'Estaing had always been highly thought of by the public. He had been considered ever since 1965 as the man with the brightest political future and was acclaimed for his competence, intelligence, and integrity. He was also a young man (just 49) and appeared to many as a "new man"; he was the only important candidate who had not held a ministerial position in the Fourth Republic. In fact, he had been elected for the first time in 1956—two years before the coming of the Fifth Republic. Many Gaullists also found it difficult to accept that their Minister of Finance for so long had been in fact a man "of the Right." Public opinion polls showed Chaban-Delmas and Giscard d'Estaing running neck to neck in the beginning. As the campaign progressed, however, the primary question in the minds of the voters was the contest on the second ballot between either Chaban-Delmas or Giscard d'Estaing against Mitterrand. Which one of the two was more likely to defeat Mitterrand? Giscard d'Estaing did not have the support of a strong party organization, and in fact, was opposed or generally ignored by the Gaullist Party. Chaban-Delmas was the candidate of the Gaullists. When the polls showed that their chances were the same, or when Giscard d'Estaing was given a better chance, the current turned irresistably in his favor.

But there were other reasons, too. The voters did not distinguish sharply between the two "majority" candidates in terms of their political attachments. In fact, more than 40 percent of the Gaullist voters saw in Giscard d'Estaing the man who would continue the policies of the majority. Further, the growing rancor of Chaban-Delmas discredited him. The victory of Giscard d'Estaing over Chaban-Delmas on the first ballot gave him something that he had lacked—electoral credibility. He entered the second ballot with the serenity and confidence that Mitterrand had displayed throughout the first and he continued it to the last day, as his opponent was beginning to lose his.

The Issues

Before we give the results of the first ballot let us survey the basic issues that seemed to separate the three major candidates—Mitterrand, Giscard d'Estaing and Chaban-Delmas. Let us also try to look briefly at the profile of their supporters. How far did these issues resemble those before the electorate in the legislative election and what were the new problems evoked and answers suggested?

The issues were more clearly stated on the first ballot than on the second. The first balloting resembled an election that is relatively polarized, with each candidate attempting to identify himself with his electoral base. At the left this was clearly the position of Mitterrand who remained by and large behind the walls of his electorate and that of the Common Program. He was guarding the leftist estate that he hoped to see enlarged but without believing it could cover half the country—not on the first ballot! Chaban-Delmas appealed chiefly to the Gaullists and portrayed Giscard d'Estaing as the spokesman of unconstructed liberal capitalism, the man of property, international capitalism, even as the Trojan horse of the American monopolies and multinationals. Michel Debré, one of the most orthodox of the Gaullists, accused the Minister of Finance of making concessions to the United States on monetary matters and perhaps of favoring Europe, at the expense of national independence. Chaban-Delmas hoped to freeze the Gaullist votes behind him and if he could come even close to the Gaullist and CDP vote in the legislative election—about 30 percent—he would be second to Mitterrand and face him in the runoff. To insure his supporters of his Gaullist credentials he repeated the slogans that had won him applause and support when he was Prime Minister. He was the advocate of the New Society—calling for a greater dialogue between Executive and Parliament, legislature and administration, administrators and administered, a greater participation of the workers, a rapid decentralization with real powers to be given at long last to regional and local entities. He brought the attack right to the doorstep of the Minister of Finance by promising to reduce the powers of the Ministry and break it up into separate units. In so doing Chaban-Delmas was not only fortifying (or hoping to fortify) his positions among the Gaullists, but was aiming to cast his opponent into the "right-wing" fortress from which there is no escape for any aspiring French political leader.

Giscard d'Estaing simply retaliated by first associating himself with Gaullism and with the "majority" he had served for so long, and second by appealing to the centrist vote. As we noted in our discussion of the legislative election, the centrist vote represents in France under optimum conditions as much as 30 percent. Remarks made by Giscard d'Estaing about introducing a modified proportional representation system, enlightened liberal economic measures and a return to a genuine European vocation were calculated to appeal to this vote. But Giscard d'Estaing could not dissociate himself from "the majority" (one of whose leaders he had been) and he outlined with pride its accomplishments, while conceding the many reforms still awaiting implementation. Economic growth in France had been among the highest in the world; the real wages of the workers had almost doubled in the last ten years; full employment was a reality, and the recent inflation was due to developments far beyond the control of France. Giscard d'Estaing defended the "majority's" record.

All the other candidates stuck to sectarian and narrow issues and searched for votes from specific groups, professions or ideological families. The "Big Three" moved very carefully from their own strong positions, trying to make occasional forays into the terrain held by the others. Chaban-Delmas and Mitterrand stood firm in defending their forces—or at least had they considered to be "their own forces." Mitterrand held them; Chaban-Delmas lost them to Giscard d'Estaing.

We shall now examine the issues and identify the positions taken by the three major candidates who, after all, received over 90 percent of the votes. They fall into three groups: institutions, foreign policy questions, and the proposed social and economic reforms. Generally, Chaban-Delmas identified himself with the Gaullist line. Giscard d'Estaing, while endorsing it, introduced modifications in line with his self-professed liberalism and Europeanism, but also in line with the general preferences of the centrist electorate. Mitterrand remained close to the Common Program of the Left. All three of them, however, put the accent on change and renewal.

INSTITUTIONS

The strongest advocate of a presidential system remained, strangely enough, Giscard d'Estaing. The President was to retain all his prerogatives and in effect "govern" through his Prime Minister and the cabinet. But he accepted the "independent prerogatives and powers of the legislature." He favored shortening the term of the presidency to five, instead of seven years. In addition, much in line with American and British systems, he wanted to create mechanisms and practices through which the "opposition" could be consulted before important decisions were taken. He advocated, like Pompidou, the formation of a new enlarged presidential majority excluding the Communists, but not necessarily the Socialists. It was to comprise, if possible, "all" but the Communists.

The Socialist leader himself was not prepared to cast any doubts about his intention to use the presidency as an instrument of political leadership. Mitterrand, too, was in favor of reducing the length of the term to five years. However, an important qualification came straight from the Common Program, concerning the right of dissolution. If, he pointed out, he were elected he would appoint a government that would have to reflect the presidential majority—that is, Communists, Socialists, Radicals of the Left and other leftists. If it were refused confidence he would dissolve and call for a new election. But after this first dissolution it would be up to the new majority to decide. In other words, he was making the Parliament and the cabinet headed by the Prime Minister the final judge of when to dissolve, thus depriving the President of an important instrument of control.

All candidates wanted changes in the electoral law. All of them promised to grant the right of vote to the younger people, beginning at 18 or 19. But while Chaban-Delmas remained faithful to the existing majoritarian electoral system, Mitterrand proposed, again in line with the Common Program, reintroducing proportional representations. Giscard d'Estaing favored also a modification of the electoral system so that important minority groups and political leaders could be given representation in the National Assembly. It is not clear what he meant but many thought that he planned to reintroduce a modified version of the German system, providing for the election of at least a fraction of the deputies by a proportional system.

All candidates favored decentralization: to give in varying degrees genuine representative institutions to the regions; they all favored extending educational opportunities for all, adult education, and modifying the processes through which access to higher education is assured.

FOREIGN POLICY

The differences among the candidates on foreign policy were not clear; matters of emphasis and degree separated them. Chaban-Delmas was the closest to the Gaullist line: nuclear force, national independence, Europeanism based on a strong and independent France, no participation in the Disarmament conference or the Conference on the Mutual Reduction of Forces in Europe, no binding consultative mechanisms with the United States, and of course good relations with the Soviet Union and the Eastern European countries. Giscard d'Estaing concurred by and large but seemed to consider constructing a political

Europe by 1980 and possibly a common European defense as high priorities. France was to remain independent but in solidarity with Europe. As for the United States, it should remain France's equal partner.

Mitterrand often sidestepped the Common Program. France would not be absent from the major conference (on disarmament and on mutual reduction of forces in Europe). On atomic weapons his position was just as Gaullist as that of anybody else. He would favor disarmament with an eye to a mutual agreement on destroying atomic weapons by those who have them. If this failed, he felt that the matter would then have to be reconsidered. He was "frankly European" and praised the Gaullist Foreign Minister for his desire to establish European institutions that would permit "Europe" to speak with one voice. But these institutions—especially the European Assembly—should be elected directly by the peoples involved so that the workers, the Trade Unions and "the masses" would be actively represented. Mitterrand was not "anti-American," he pointed out. He grudgingly conceded the necessity of the Atlantic "alliance" but pointed out that French national independence was not a matter to be bargained about. His most critical remarks were about the penetration of American capital in the European market and the role of the multinational corporations. Finally, all candidates came out firmly for the integrity and security of Israel. Chaban-Delmas went so far as to advocate the lifting of the embargo of arms. Giscard d'Estaing frowned upon the competition for the sale of arms and suggested an Israel–Arab conference and a possible equilibrium of forces there. Mitterrand expressed his deep "sympathy" for Israel. All three also emphasized the good relations between France and the Arab world.

WHAT KIND OF SOCIETY? SOCIAL AND ECONOMIC ISSUES

It would be impossible to do justice to the specific pledges made by the candidates with regard to economic and social changes and reforms. First, because notwithstanding all appearances to the contrary, the differences were rather marginal and often made by insinuation, especially if we exclude, as we did for the legislative elections, the nationalizations of certain economic activities advocated by Mitterrand. There was some irony in this. From the very start the election was supposed to offer a choice between two types of society, two ways of life. Presented in the broadest possible ideological terms, it was the choice between continuing a capitalist society—portrayed by the Left as inhuman, selfish, based upon the interest of a few, perpetuating exploitation in the form of vast inequalities, welcoming foreign investment and especially American ones, insensitive to the qualitative dimensions of life, bent upon economic growth for the sake of growth and insensitive to the liberal traditions of France as the champion of freedom and of the underprivileged in this world. On the other side there was the idyllic picture of Socialism as it was about to develop, subordinating private interest to the public one; moving ahead to nationalize major corporations, bent upon egalitarianism and internal prosperity, sheltering the French economy from foreign international marauders, spreading the gospel of liberty and equality abroad.

"Politics is ideas," an eminent French writer proclaimed. There is no doubt that the ideological juxtaposition mobilized the French and deeply involved them in the election. It evoked attitudes, inclinations, images and affinities that go back to the French Revolution: the past against the present; progress against the status quo; equality against privilege, popular participation against a political class that had held power for so long and had found ways to propagate itself in power; patriotism and independence against foreign capital; the integrity of French values and way of life against Americanization (or, rather, industrialization); the little man against the bureaucrat and the peasant against the landowner.

But what about the position of the candidates? Both Chaban-Delmas and Giscard d'Estaing emphasized change. The first argued for a "new society"; the second for "continuity *and* change." Chaban-Delmas advocated the "third way" between Socialism and capitalism in the form of the old Gaullist plan of associating fully the workers in the profits of the firms. He promised to increase expenditure in the social sectors—hospitals, schools, public transports. He stated time after time that the national revenue should be distributed more equitably among various groups in an effort to reduce income disparities. He argued for regionalization so that the economic plan and regional development, but many other issues as well, could be decided by those immediately concerned. He advocated reducing indirect taxes and increasing income taxes; he favored the increases in the real purchasing power of the salaried, a minimum monthly salary of about $220, and equality in pay between men and women. He promised half a million new jobs in thirty months, better and cheaper medical care, and higher family allowances.

Giscard d'Estaing put the emphasis on continuing economic growth—at least 5 percent per year—and redistributing its benefits in a more equitable fashion. He too emphasized social services, reducing inequalities in income (in fact, he promised that the low salaries should increase twice as fast as the higher ones), and of course equality in the pay of men and women. He pledged, too, to lower indirect taxes but otherwise he was hostile to any increase in taxation; he hoped, as we noted, that the advantages of economic growth would benefit the needier. He went beyond Chaban-Delmas in promising reforms in the social security system. He called for a "Charter for mothers," aid to widows, and the handicapped, and in general across-the-board increase in family allowances and family aid, and cheaper and better medical service for all. He pledged a minimum monthly pension of about $125.00 per month for the aged and increasing the minimum wage to about $220.00 per month. He refused, however, to consider nationalizations or any major structural reforms fearing that they might undermine the momentum the French economy had gained. "We must modify and improve the economic instrument we have," not "break it."

Mitterrand appeared the most reformist of the three. He proposed two short-term plans, the first for six months and the second for eighteen months, and then a major five-year plan. The purpose was to develop economic growth geared to qualitative considerations, to reduce the inequalities and allow the workers to participate in the decisions of the firms. The plan should allow for full decentralization giving autonomy to the public firms and the local and regional units. He promised to expand the public sector thanks to the nationalization of nine major industrial groups. He suggested measures to stop inflation, by price controls and exchange controls. He promised to cut indirect taxes sharply. The minimum monthly salary was to be raised to $225, with a cost of living index and the pay of civil servants was to be raised. An allowance of about $180.00 a month was to be provided for young people who were seeking employment. He, too, asked for better and cheaper medical services, increase in the help to the aged and handicapped, the increase in the old age pension to about $125 a month and the right to retire at the age of 60.

The First Ballot

The first ballot indicated the high interest of the voters in presidential elections and demonstrated the stability of voting patterns both by geographic regions and political families. Yet it was within the major families that shifts occurred. As Table 4–2 above shows, 84 percent of the registered voters went to the polls, a percentage surpassed only in the presidential election of 1965. As for stability, the election appeared on its face as an unprecedented triumph of the Union of the Left. The vote for Mitterrand alone—representing Communists, Socialists, Radicals of the Left and PSU—amounted to 43.2 percent. On the first ballot of the presidential election of 1965 Mitterrand had received just about 32 percent; in 1969 the combined vote of a disunited dispirited Left was also just about 32 percent. He now led with 43.2 percent. But when we compare Mitterrand's score to the 1973 legislative election we find that the parties Mitterrand represented had received 44.1 percent of the vote, so that Mitterrand's forces had in fact lost but only about 1 percent. Only if we include *all* the leftist candidates do we find that the Left *as a whole* had bettered its overall score, but by no more than 1 percent. Stability remained the rule.

Only detailed analysis will indicate transfers in the voting patterns of the French, reinforcing some of the trends we observed in our discussion of the legislative election. We shall indicate here the major dimensions of the voting trends only. First, the Socialist electorate as a whole did not follow Mitterrand as fully as expected. As many as one million voters—3 percent and more—voted for either the majority candidates, Giscard d'Estaing or Chaban-Delmas, or for others. A number of Communists too abandoned Mitterrand in favor of another candidate, but their percentage was relatively much smaller. How did then Mitterrand come so close to the combined vote of the leftist parties that supported him in 1973? Simply because there was an equivalent transfer from centrist and even Gaullist voters to him. This becomes clear by looking at the regions where the Socialist vote had been relatively weak; in these areas Mitterrand gained appreciably. In the areas where the Communist and Socialist position had been strong, however, Mitterrand just about held to the vote of 1973 and often fell behind. In Alsace he gained 9 points; in Lorraine almost 6 points; in Normandy about 4 points. Yet he fell behind in the strongholds of the Left: the region of the Nord where he lost 5 points; in Provence, 2 points; in Limousin 4½ points; in Auvergne almost 4 points. There was a slight displacement, fewer than a million votes, to Mitterrand from the Center and the Gaullists. This compensated roughly—but not quite—for his losses from the transfer of Leftist voters to other candidates and notably Giscard d'Estaing or Chaban-Delmas. Would the same voters be lost to him on the second ballot? Would the centrists return to the centrist fold? Given the closeness of the vote, the outcome was to be decided by small shifts that, given the personal factor so important in presidential elections, may well defy any careful sociological analysis.

The most dramatic aspect of the election was the collapse of the Gaullist candidate, Chaban-Delmas. With less than 15 percent of the vote he fell far behind the corresponding votes of DeGaulle and Pompidou in the previous presidential elections. He also hardly managed to get half the votes that were cast for the two parties he represented, the Gaullists and the CDP, in the legislative election of 1973. There were several reasons for this collapse. First, the Gaullist voters felt close to Giscard d'Estaing who had been a member of the majority and a Minister of Finance for so long. Second, the attacks of Chaban-Delmas against Giscard d'Estaing and his efforts to pin the latter on the Right while claiming himself to be in the Center were not taken seriously. Thus he lost votes among both the Gaullists and the Center. But the major explanation lies in the revival of the Center as a political family under the leadership of the only man who could unite it while biting hard into the Gaullist vote.

It was this revival of the Center in alliance with the Gaullist votes that constitutes the major and possibly most significant development of the election. In 1965 the centrist candidate for the presidency, Lecanuet, received about 15 percent of the vote. In 1969 another centrist candidate reached a high of 23 percent, but the Left was split and many Socialists had voted for the centrist. In 1974 Giscard d'Estaing received 33 percent, coming far ahead of his Gaullist opponent. His own party had accounted for 7 percent in the legislative election, and the *Réformateurs* for 12.5 percent. The rest was made up from the voters that abandoned the Gaullist candidate to return to the centrist fold. However, the Center-Right vote fell from 59 percent in the presidential election of 1965 and as much as 67 percent in 1969 to not more than 53 percent in 1974. In fact, the combined vote of all centrists and Gaullist candidates was almost identical with the score of the URP and the *Réformateurs* put together in the legislative election of 1973.

It was a non-Gaullist, then, who faced Mitterrand in the runoff. Would the bulk of the centrist vote stay behind him, and would those who strayed to the Left return? More especially, would the Gaullists who voted for Chaban-Delmas vote for him? Or would they abstain or even vote for Mitterrand? And what about the new voters who might vote on the second ballot having abstained on the first?

The sociology of the electorate was markedly similar to the one we observed in the legislative election. While a majority of men voted for Mitterrand, women gave their support to Giscard d'Estaing and Chaban-Delmas. Younger people clustered behind Mitterrand, but older voters leaned toward Giscard d'Estaing and Chaban-Delmas. At least 60 percent of the farmers voted for Giscard d'Estaing (38 percent) and Chaban-Delmas (23 percent). Only 21 percent of the workers went for Giscard d'Estaing and only 9 percent to Chaban-Delmas (an obvious indication that the Gaullist candidate was unable to get the worker support he claimed). Yet the two together on the first ballot accounted *for 30 percent* of the workers in the electorate. Those inactive were solidly behind the Gaullist and centrist candidates, including Royer. As for the party voters, three and four out of every hundred Communists were to vote for Giscard d'Estaing and Chaban-Delmas respectively; eight and four out of every hundred Socialists; 58 and 12 out of the *Réformateurs;* and 56 and 29 out of the "majority." The sociological profile of the voters as well as the geographic distribution of the vote followed closely the previous patterns and was to be sharply delineated despite transfers on the second ballot (see Table 4–3).

TABLE 4–3: SOCIOLOGICAL AND POLITICAL PROFILE OF VOTERS BASED ON INTENTIONS TO VOTE WITH 13% UNDECIDED

Distribution	Giscard d'Estaing %	Mitterrand %
Overall	50	50
Men	47	53
Women	52	48
Age		
21–34 years	44	56
35–49 years	49	51
50–64 years	48	52
65 and above	62	38
Occupation of Head of Household		
Liberal professions and top managerial personnel	72	28
Entrepreneurs, commerce and industry	63	37
Salaried and white collar	51	49
Workers	29	71
Inactive (retired, student, etc.)	58	42
Farmers	66	34
Residence		
Rural communes	54	46
Towns of less than 20,000	49	51
20,000–100,000	51	49
More than 100,000	58	52
Paris region	45	55
Political Preferences		
Communist Party	5	95
Non-Communist Left (Socialist Party [PS], Unified Socialist Party [PSU], Radicals of the Left)	12	88
Réformateurs	75	25
Majority (Gaullists, Independent Republicans – CDP)	88	12
Voted on First Ballot for		
Chaban-Delmas	86	14
Giscard d'Estaing	96	4
Mitterrand	3	97
Royer	78	22
Extreme Left	18	82

Source: France-Soir, May 16, 1974. This is a survey of the Institut Français d'Opinion Publique.

The Second Ballot

To analyze the nature of the ten day campaign between Giscard d'Estaing and Mitterrand on the second ballot we must again distinguish clearly between verbal ideological pronouncement and actual political tactics. The manichean distinction between the inherent goodness of the candidate of the Left and the wickedness of their adversary was maintained to the bitter end. Giscard d'Estaing was dubbed as the candidate of the Right. Every effort was made to pin him down as an ally of capitalism, associated with banks and monied interests, multinational corporations, insensitive to the problems of the workers and the little man. Since he had been Minister of Finance for almost eight years in the Gaullist regime, he was to be blamed for the inequalities of the system. He was portrayed as being far more conservative than the Gaullists ever had been. It was even argued that he hailed from those who had supported the Vichy regime that had collaborated with the Germans in World War II. His Europeanism was also seen as a sure sign that national independence might soon be drowned into what DeGaulle had called an *"apatride* Europe"—that is, a Europe without nation-states.

Suddenly the Gaullists—whom the Communists and Mitterrand had fought bitterly ever since 1958—became the darlings of the Left as they tried to take as many voters of Chaban-Delmas away from Giscard d'Estaing as possible. In a timely book, "When We Were Ministers," serialized in the daily Communist paper, the old-time Communist leader, François Billoux, reminded the French that the Communists had cooperated with DeGaulle and had participated in his cabinet. They had shown patriotism, abnegation, the highest respect for service and efficiency in the Ministries they occupied—all for the good of the country and the resurrection of French power. When it came to the crucial issues —the resistance to the Nazis, restoring France's independence, defeating the project to establish a European integrated army, resisting American pressures, the independence of Algeria—the Communists and the Gaullists had fought side by side. This election they claimed would once more decide the independence and the well-being of France. What could stop patriots like Communists and Gaullists from cooperating? Chaban-Delmas, who had been assiduously attacked by the Communists in the past, became now an object of pity and affection; his electoral flock (15 percent of the voters) became an object of the most intense solicitation.

Giscard d'Estaing answered in kind by attempting to identify his opponent with the Communists and thus gain Centrist and even Socialist votes. The candidate of the Left was called the prisoner of the Communists. He was the "socialo-communist" candidate, favoring a collectivist and bureaucratic society. He would, as it happened so often in other countries, be swallowed by the huge Communist party machine. To have Communist Ministers in the government was "irresponsible." Somehow Giscard d'Estaing managed to convey the impression that though the Communist voters—more than five million strong—were good Frenchmen they were the dupes of the leadership whose ultimate aim was to establish a collectivist society and destroy the French economy. Giscard d'Estaing promised a change of the society "without risks," as opposed to the risk of profound social upheavals.

But he vehemently rejected all efforts to bind him to a "right-wing" faction. He was the architect of one of the fastest growing economies in Europe. And it was time now to move forward and equalize opportunities and reduce inequalities, without breaking the rhythm of growth. Nationalizations and collectivizations could destroy the industrial machinery of the country. But he introduced a new note—the note of a new France—liberated from the clichés of the past, shedding ideological controversies, moving on with intelligent political leadership to manipulate the economy in order to serve the interests of the whole. The time for old time political rhetoric was over; the time was to do things and accomplish new projects. Giscard d'Estaing, the youngest candidate, had the best educational background and technical experience. He too was pleading for a new society. As for the flirtation between Gaullists and Communists—even if one-sided—Giscard d'Estaing meant to put an end to it. His party had formed part of the "majority" for fourteen years. He had cooperated personally with General DeGaulle. And even if on occasion he had disagreed with him, he had remained loyal to him and his governments. Even if not a Gaullist he had been as close to them as anybody else and indeed one of the most influential political leaders within the majority.

The Gaullist party, deeply depressed over the electoral collapse of its leader, was reluctantly forced into the open again. They could not tolerate the Communist insinuations of a *rapprochement* with their voters. Though some of its leaders sulked and a few mavericks went out to urge a vote for Mitterrand, the Party could not allow for a situation to develop in which either out of apathy and discouragement or because of the left-wing solicitations Gaullist voters would either abstain or vote for the candidate of the "socialo-communists." One by one the wounded leaders came out and spoke either against Mitterrand or for Giscard d'Estaing. Yet the Gaullist party as such never gave its full support to Giscard d'Estaing did not organize meetings for him; did not provide for publicity and funds. Only in the last big rally two days before the election did Gaullist dignitaries share the same podium with Giscard d'Estaing. But by then, given the expected closeness of the vote, they had no choice.

In contrast the Communists gave their full and unflinching support to Mitterrand. Every day, while the two candidates flew from one to another city of France, the Communists worked the grassroots. They organized hundreds of meetings, mobilized their voters, provided for full newspaper coverage (in their national newspaper as well as many local ones), used their Trade Union contracts to stir up support among the doubtful workers, and threw timely invectives against the "candidate of the reaction." In the process, and in the hope of getting the uncertain voters and at least a fraction of the Gaullists, they began to pour water in their wine. They accepted the presidential system fully. Mitterrand was to be free to develop his own policies and to select his Prime Minister. They were not against his appointing to the cabinet political leaders who might have opposed them. They would not demand any of the key Ministries in the cabinet, such as Defense, Interior or Foreign Affairs. While remaining faithful to the Common Program, they understood very well that it was up to the President and his cabinet to decide about the timing of its implementation!

It is unnecessary to speculate on the real motives of the Communist party. Winning the election was for them both a means and an end. The end was access to the government and therefore the respectability to be gained by cooperating faithfully with Mitterrand and the new majority in gradually implementing the Common Program. The means was simply in the nature of "wait and see." Once in the government and in control of Ministerial posts, they could, depending upon the circumstances, decide on their tactics. The proverbial rope they extended to Mitterrand could be used not only to hang him, as many hinted, but also to support him. And Mitterrand, no novice in the game of politics, and especially Socialist-Communist relations, was fully aware of the dangers and opportunities deriving from Communist support. Elected President he could revive the Socialist party and make the Socialists again the first party of France. Whatever the respective motives, however, cooperation for the election was intimate. The Communists and Mitterrand remained fully loyal to each other.

Many of the above issues and some related ones came to a head in the televised debate between Mitterrand and Giscard d'Estaing. The debate lasted one hour and was watched by over twenty million Frenchmen. The occasion showed—and the polls confirmed this later—that the presidential election system by direct franchise is overwhelmingly accepted in France by as many as 85 percent of the public. But it also showed, from the very first words spoken by the two candidates, that one of the Gaullist legacies we discussed earlier is likely to cause problems: Giscard d'Estaing calmly and confidently pointed out to Mitterrand that if he were elected, there was a majority in the National Assembly consisting of all centrists and Gaullists—the majority emanating from the 1973 election—that would be favorable to him. It would be a "new majority" in the sense that it would include the *Réformateurs* —both of whose leaders came out for Giscard d'Estaing and received Ministerial posts—and therefore a more solid one. Giscard d'Estaing claimed some 300 votes out of 490. What would his opponent do if he won? This is the dilemma in which the Gaullists have put their opponent ever since 1965. In that year it was pointed out that if DeGaulle lost, his opponent (Mitterrand) would have to face a hostile Assembly. In 1973 the same argument was inverted: if the legislative election produced a leftist majority it would pit itself against a Gaullist President —Pompidou. In 1974 it was a repeat of the 1965 situation. It is an argument that created a dilemma for the voters. In either case—whether they vote for a President who does not have a majority support in the National Assembly (1965, 1969 and 1974) or for a majority in the National Assembly that is against the incumbent President (1962 and 1973) —they may bring about a potential political crisis that is likely to call for a new election. Many voters fearful of such crisis prefer to vote for the status quo. In this sense Mitterrand was clear in his answer to Giscard d'Estaing in the televised debate: if the Assembly did not vote confidence in his Prime Minister and cabinet he would dissolve and call for a new election.

Another topic discussed during the debate was the participation of the Communists in the government in the context of a binding "Common Program." Mitterrand declared that the Communists were French men and women and they could not be excluded forever from political participation. Would Giscard d'Estaing amputate almost a quarter of the French from the national community? Giscard d'Estaing would not, but neither would he have them in the government. He did not consider them as "foreign agents" but he had severe doubts about letting them participate in government decisions and share government secrets.

The third major topic of debate was, of course, the economy. Here the same generalizations were repeated. On the one hand, there was a collectivist plan, bound to undermine France's position in the international economy, to arrest growth, to make French products less competitive and perhaps ultimately to force France into a position of protectionism. Giscard d'Estaing planned to finance significant social reforms through economic growth by making the pie of the national product bigger, rather than to follow a Malthusian policy of keeping the pie the same and cutting it into different slices. Nationalizations were no longer an adequate instrument of economic development and growth. "You are a man of the past," he said to his opponent, and this was to become the theme of his campaign. "You think of the past; you analyze situations in terms of past occurrences. I am thinking of the future. Let us talk about the future." Later on Giscard d'Estaing said that the candidate of the Left was retrogressing. First it is the Resistance (1941–1944), then the Popular Front (1936), "now," he claimed, "he invokes the French Revolution" (1789). "Soon he will be fighting the battle of Poitiers (732)." "I can't catch up with him." The remark hit a sensitive spot. Mitterrand—ten years older than his opponent—had been eleven times Minister under the despised Fourth Republic. His vocabulary, his tone, his allusions and illustrations "smelled" of the past.

The counterattack took several forms, but the most persistent ones were that 1. Giscard d'Estaing was the lackey of the monied interests and the upper bourgeoisie; and 2. that he was responsible for the situation in the country, having been Minister of Finance for so long. The Socialist and Communist newspapers ran series of pictures showing the "candidate of the Right" in his various chateaux; they accused him of buying large estates, and traced his ancestry to show that drops of despicable royal blood were mingled with some of the most reactionary poison. The campaign was getting "animated" and Giscard d'Estaing had to bring forward the names of Roosevelt and Kennedy—patricians and millionaires—who stood for left-wing policies and reform.

The sharpness of the debate emphasized also the personalization of the election. The citizen was judging the man, not the program. Even on the Left (despite the Communist emphasis on the Common Program) only 47 percent of the voters said they would vote for a program and not the man. There is no doubt that Giscard d'Estaing, not bound to a program or to any large political party, appeared to be his own man.

In two radio interviews the two candidates dealt with foreign policy questions. Giscard d'Estaing mindful of the Gaullist vote, came out openly now for continuing the Pompidou foreign policy. He now accepted everything—*force de frappe,* continuations of nuclear tests, the absence of France from the two major international conferences on the Mutual Reduction of Forces in Europe and on disarmament, "national independence" and collaboration with all on the basis of equality and, of course, the Atlantic alliance and the stationing of U.S. troops in Europe. The new note—but not so new—was the urgency for the construction of Europe. Mitterrand began to qualify the original positions he had taken before the first ballot. He disavowed any intention of doing away with the *force de frappe* or the Atlantic alliance, as long as there was no alternative system of defense. "As the head of the French state I cannot jeopardize the protection of France." He evoked the Gaullist commitment to national independence but he, too, seemed committed to Europe. Yet he stressed that to attain independence France must rid itself of foreign economic dependence, and particularly American controls—direct or indirect—over the French economy.

Little seemed to separate the two candidates, and the consensus was that foreign policy did not play a role in the election. In public opinion polls Mitterrand scored high on his reformist policy, his sensitivity to the needs of the poor and underprivileged and his understanding of their problems. But Giscard d'Estaing was considered the best candidate "to represent the interests of France in the world." DeGaulle's foreign policy had been approved by the people. Giscard d'Estaing represented a continuity for many voters; Mitterrand was an unknown.

The debate on the large options was only a part of the electoral contest. The major part was the "nitty-gritty" of politics: how to get the votes. The two candidates, trying to get the marginals and the undecided (about 12–14 percent before the second ballot), began to sound alike and often cross into each other's territory. There was a daily avalanche of pledges made by both, not on overall issues but on details. Youth associations, the aged, those living on pensions, wives and young mothers, the fishermen, the ecologists, the white collar workers associations, the holders of Russian bonds (some 15 billion gold francs had been invested—and lost when the Bolsheviks came to power), individual leaders were all given audience. Promises were made to all—promises that began to sound very much alike.

In the process the programmatic commitments were qualified. It was not a matter of introducing nationalizations right away, conceded Mitterrand. Giscard d'Estaing began to have second thoughts on changing the electoral system along the lines he had suggested earlier. Mitterrand produced a charter of the "Third (Old) Age" but one of the very first acts of his opponent was to promise to increase old age pensions and reduce the age of retirement. He reiterated his promise to increase the minimum wages, provide for controls in real estate speculation, build more housing units, reduce the voting age to perhaps 18 or 19, reduce indirect taxes, provide for better hospitals, increase social security benefits, and so on. The promises amounted to a social package that in no way could come from a candidate of "the Right," and differed little from the specifics advanced by Mitterrand. As with the legislative election of 1973, despite the overall ideological symbolisms that seemed to entail a choice between two fundamentally different ways of life, the specifics showed a remarkable degree of convergence: to modify gradually the status quo, to reduce inequalities, to humanize the harshness of the industrial society, to maintain employment and to provide for greater security, equal opportunities for all and leisure. The allegedly polarized election was in essence a highly competitive one. Both candidates were out to get out the vote, spreading their net as wide as possible to catch as many undecided as they could.

The Results

The phenomenon we observed with the legislative election of 1973 was repeated. The candidate of the Left who had come so comfortably ahead of all others on the first ballot was defeated because of the concentration of the Right-Center voters against him. But it was closer than ever before. With about 900,000 more voters than on the first ballot —a record participation—Giscard d'Estaing won with 50.8 percent against 49.2 percent for Mitterrand. Less than 1.5 percent separated the two candidates—400,000 votes. The overseas departments and territories did not make any significant difference; they gave Giscard d'Estaing an edge of about 20,000 votes. The victory, narrow as it was, had been won in France. The Left held to its votes and managed to get back a good part of those who had gone astray on the first ballot. Mitterrand received only fractions of the votes of the centrists and of Chaban-Delmas and Royer, and this was not enough. More than 88 percent of the voters of Chaban-Delmas went to Giscard d'Estaing and as many as 70 percent of Royer's. In addition a very small percentage of the leftist vote—not more than 2–3 percent—went to Giscard d'Estaing. Everywhere the Left gained, but not enough; everywhere the Right-Center lost, but not enough.

In comparison to the legislative election of 1973, the Left as a whole gained about 3 percent. They barely held the leftist vote in the 162 electoral districts that they had carried in 1973; however, they gained more than 11 percent in all districts that had been won by the *Réformateurs* and over 5 percent in all districts that had been won by the "majority." (See Table 4-4.)

In contrast, Giscard d'Estaing mobilized fully the Gaullist and centrist vote where the Left was strong. But he lost, sometimes heavily, in the areas that had been won in the legislative election by a "centrist" or a "majority" candidate. The vote for Giscard d'Estaing shows an overall decline of the Center-Right vote that corresponds to the 2–3 percent gain of the Left, both with regard to the combined total of Center-Gaullist candidates on the first ballot of the presidential election and the legislative election of 1973. He just barely managed to hold on to a very slim majority. It was a victory that many interpreted to be the harbinger of a "majoritarian" Left.

Both the sociological profile of the voters and the geographic distribution of the vote remained familiar, despite the relative gains of Mitterrand. The distribution by age, sex, and occupation shows the electorate of Giscard d'Estaing to be feminine (but the difference is somewhat deceptive since there are about 16 million women of age to vote in France as opposed to 14,200,000 men). The major difference occurs in the age groups above 65, in which there are about 2,600,000 men as opposed to 4,200,000 women. This age group went as much as 6.5 out of 10 for Giscard d'Estaing. The new President was not supported by the workers; not more than twenty out of every hundred actual voters for Giscard d'Estaing were workers. In absolute terms, out of about 8 million workers not more than 2 million of *all* the workers voted for Giscard d'Estaing. On its face it was an election that seemed to revive again the traditional class vote even more than the legislative election of 1973.

TABLE 4–4: COMPARISON OF STRENGTH OF LEFT IN 1973 LEGISLATIVE ELECTIONS AND VOTES OBTAINED BY MITTERRAND IN 1974 ELECTION

Party of Winning Deputy Candidate	1973 Left	1974 d'Estaing	Mitterrand
In 73 electoral districts with a Communist winner the Left averaged	58.6%	41.5%	58.5%
In 89 electoral districts with a Socialist winner the Left averaged	55.1	44.8	55.2
In 32 electoral districts with a *Réformateur* winner the Left averaged	33.6	55.4	44.6
In 257 electoral districts with a "majority" winner the Left averaged	39.3	55.1	44.9

Source: Le Point, May 21, 1974.

All big cities—but not Paris and the Paris region (he won by 0.4 percent)—went appreciably for Mitterrand but with some notable exceptions. The younger groups (below 45) voted also in greater numbers for Mitterrand. Giscard d'Estaing carried a majority (fifty-one) of all departments. He gained over 60 percent in eleven. His opponent received a majority in forty-four departments with 60 percent and over in nine. The juxtaposition of the following electoral maps indicate the most remarkable stability in the voting patterns between Left and Center-Right. The New Gaul seems to be divided into two!

Figure 1: Referendum of May 5, 1946

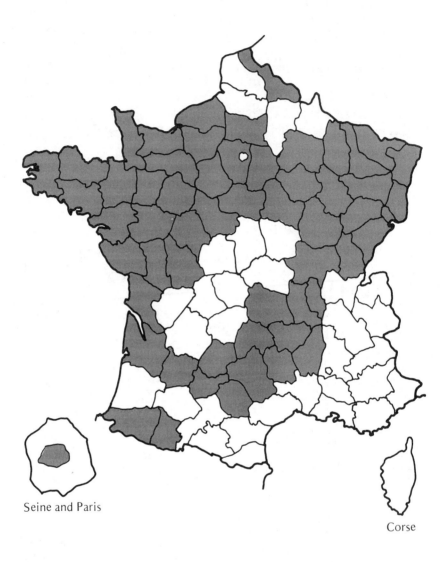

Seine and Paris

Corse

In grey, those voting against (49% and over) the constitutional text submitted
(Right, Right Center and Centrist voters).

Source: Adapted from François Goguel's *Géographie des Elections Françaises sous la
Troisième et la Quatrième Republique* (Armand Colin, 1970).

Figure 2: Election of April 26, 1936

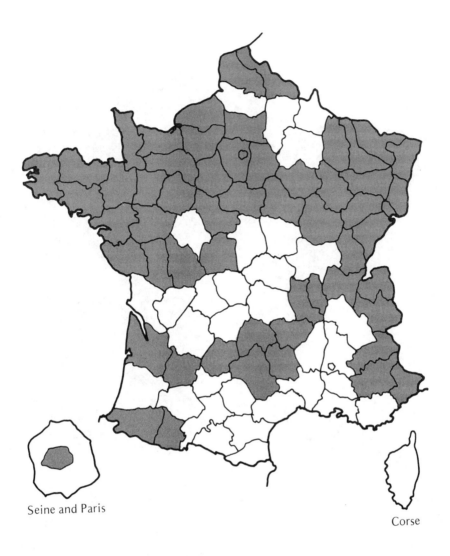

Seine and Paris

Corse

In grey, those voting against (49% and over) the Popular Front Coalition (Right, (Right, Right Center and Centrist voters).

Source: Ibid.

Figure 3: Presidential Election of May 19, 1974

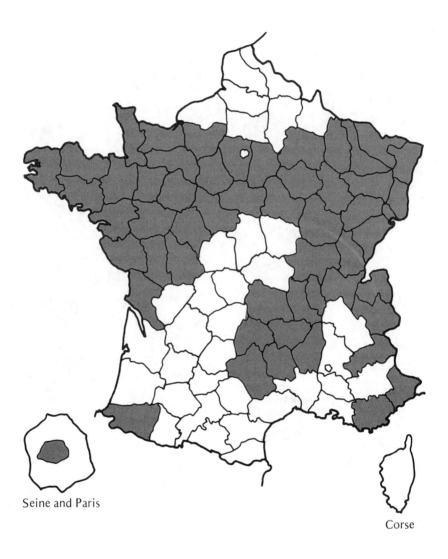

Seine and Paris

Corse

In grey, those voting for (49% and over) Giscard d'Estaing and against the candidate of the United Left.

Source: Adapted from *Le Monde*, May 21, 1974.

An Overall Evaluation

Both the legislative and the presidential election held within a period of about a year show certain similarities. First, there is the remarkable return to the traditional voting patterns along geographic lines. The comparisons we gave with the election of 1936 and 1946 (Figures 1, 2 and 3) can be multiplied to include other elections even before. Second, there is a reappearance of "class" politics, at least in the sense that 75 percent of all workers seem to have voted for Mitterrand —a higher working class percentage than that of the Labour Party in Britain or the Social-Democrats in West Germany. Gaullism as a phenomenon that cuts across political families and classes seems to be no longer a factor or a force. Third, no matter where one wishes to place Giscard d'Estaing on the Left-Center-Right continuum, there is no doubt that on the second ballot the Center and Right (with some minor defections) joined forces. Does this mean that the Center moved to the Right or that in fact the differences between the two "families" became increasingly indistinguishable? Are we to see in it a possible merger or the formation of a coalition, something like the British Conservative Party? The Communist party seems to have moved out of its seclusion for good to become a party with governmental aspirations. In this respect the dynamism of the Left reached a new level of unity. All Leftist families except some minuscule extremists joined forces behind Mitterrand. Are we permitted to conclude that an integration of all Leftists (and the Communist, too) in one large political coalition is likely? Is it possible to think of the French "Left" as about to evolve into a Labor Party—proposing reforms and assuming the task of governing within the system, becoming a domesticated and assimilated Left? Finally, presidentialism with direct elections has captured the imagination of the French and it is there to stay.

Another general observation relates to the Right-Center-Left continuum. If we accept the self-imposed and self-invoked labels, the geographic continuity of the vote is astounding. But is the Left that voted for the Constitutional text of 1946 and for the Popular Front in 1936 the same as the 49 percent who gave their votes to Mitterrand in 1974? And, conversely, is the Right-Center represented on the second ballot by Giscard d'Estaing the same as those who opposed the Popular Front (and gained just as slim a majority of the popular vote on the first ballot as Giscard d'Estaing did) and who opposed the first draft of the Constitution of 1946? It is very doubtful! In fact, the only reason to use the Left-Right label is simply to label the two movements that confronted each other instead of other labels like Labor vs. Conservatives, Social Democrats vs. Christian Democrats, even Republicans vs. Democrats. They are convenient labels. It is very hard to contend that Giscard d'Estaing's electoral pledges—already in the process of implementation —correspond to the policies advocated by the traditional Right. It is equally untrue to contend, unless we insist on the nationalization program, that the Left, having fully accepted the norms of the democratic game, and with specific pledges that hardly distinguish it from the so-called Right, is the same Left that hailed from the Commune and the Popular Front or even from among the anti-clerical forces so active during the turn of the century. As with the legislative election, the labels stuck by being constantly used. But the content had changed.

What about class politics? We must again make the same distinction we made in connection with the legislative election. Class struggle has been seriously qualified; the rules of democracy accepted; the prospects of bowing to national suffrage conceded. The Communists accepted it; the Trade Unions did likewise. What is left of class politics, therefore, and what appears to be in the process of crystallizing, is the attachment of the working class to its two parties—Communists and Socialists—as the spokesmen of their interests and aspirations. In fact, the jubilation of the Left after the election was an indication of this trend. With over 49 percent of the vote, victory they asserted could not elude them again. Hence their major effort in the future may well be geared to electioneering and political organization. This is in tune with the interests of the majority of the salaried people, including workers in France. They wish to improve what has been gained; they desire no revolutionary adventures. So while class identification with the Communists and the Socialists appears to wax, class struggle and class confrontation appears to be on the wane. Already some hints were made about creating a special "status for the Opposition," in which case the distinction between "Opposition" and "Government" may well replace the Left-Center-Right categories. Elections may shed gradually their ideological residues, to deal with concrete policy packages exactly like the specific pledges made by the two candidates. It is significant that after the election, the virus of the "nationalization" program was isolated as one that may well have been the cause for Mitterrand's defeat. The Common Program, it is agreed, must be brought up to date.

And what about Gaullism? It no longer seems in the person of Giscard d'Estaing—to whom the Gaullists rallied—destined to perform the unifying role of cutting across classes and political families. But the personal aspects of the presidential election will continue to be a factor and may play that role. Some 14 percent of the voters could not decide until the very end. A slim majority among them voted for Giscard d'Estaing because of his personal qualities. There is no reason why the personality factor, without DeGaulle, may not play an important role. At least three-quarters of the voters were voting for the candidate; many did so to be sure, because of the political families they associated him with but quite a few because of his personality. Courage, experience, intelligence, competence and national representativeness were often mentioned by the voters.

But if presidentialism is likely to continue and the personality factor to play an important role in the future, the same is not the case with the real victim of the election—the Gaullist party. Their candidate lost more than half of the votes that his supporting parties received in the legislative election. It was natural to expect the defection of the centrists, the CDP, who had joined the Gaullists in 1969. Many of its voters went back to the fold they had abandoned. But what accounts for the rest? The answer lies in the very composition of the Gaullist party and its spectacular development since 1962 that we discussed earlier. It was the result of conversions from among centrists, independents and local notables. More than 40 percent of its voters came from these groups together with a small fraction from the Left. In 1974 they found in Giscard d'Estaing a candidate with whom they identified. When the Gaullist leader began to attack him they simply switched back into the centrist fold. The Leftist voters, mostly workers, who had responded to DeGaulle's appeal and who later voted for Pompidou returned, too, to their left-wing parties—the Communists or the Socialists. Thus the Gaullist party found itself amputated while the Center recovered the positions it held until as late as 1958. The title of Table 3-5, Polarization and the "Centrist Vocation," best indicates the generalization we can make about the presidential election. France seems to be moving toward two large bloc or coalition parties: Left vs. Center-Right, or "Opposition" vs. "Government." Presidential and legislative elections are likely to follow this division. The quest for victory will intensify competition and make the two blocs catch-all formations.

The elections, then, speak eloquently for the emergence of a new political situation in France. It is one (and it has been so since 1962) where majority governments are likely to be the rule and where the choice between two broad sets of policy options will be open to the electorate. The system is likely therefore to generate a stable government, committed to a program and able to count upon the support of a majority and to govern for a given length of time. As long as there is congruence between the President and a majority in the National Assembly, the Executive will be able to govern, to plan, and to implement the broad options agreed upon by the electorate.

It is difficult not to qualify some of these conclusions. We cannot eliminate the possibility, for instance, that the Communist party, threatened by a resurgent Socialist party and new extreme leftist movements, may not revert to some of its old ways, especially if the international situation changes. But if this were to happen the Socialists would be the first to move out of their alliance with the Communists and to even support the Right-Center coalition as they did in the past. Just as the Socialists are tied to the Communists for electoral purposes, so is Communist behavior heavily mortgaged by the fear of a Socialist defection. Nor can we exclude the possibility that the centrist groups, unable to form a stable coalition, may break up into a number of small parties. We cannot even exclude the hypothesis that the Gaullists may refuse to support the new President for fear of being swallowed by a centrist coalition and attempt to maintain the identity and the image of their party, faithful to the Gaullist heritage. In other words, since coalition politics are inherently unstable the disintegration of the existing two major coalitions into three—the Communists and Socialists, the centrists, and the Gaullists—or into four and more is not impossible. We shall return to this subject in our last chapter.

chapter five

Beyond Gaullism:
What Kind of State
for What Kind of Society

The legislative and presidential elections we discussed seem to have intensified some of the special traits of the French political culture: the search for overall conceptions about life and justice and happiness and for definitive solutions to society's problems. French politics continue to be intensely ideological in this sense. But the ideologies no longer fragment the body politic. They seem rather to divide it into two coalitions that for lack of a better term we have called the "Left" and the "Center-Right." This division no longer splits France into two irreconcilable camps. It is rather a division that structures and organizes opinion and the voters. Most of the old dividing ideologies are on the wane: capitalism vs. socialism; religious and private vs. lay schools, revolution vs. reform, and the individual vs. the state. Today's pressing issues relate to the distribution of the national income, to the role of France in the world, to qualitative considerations in industrial societies and the manner in which the individuals will be allowed to shape their destinies and their lives. Will it be through a powerful highly centralized State or on a pluralistic basis?

What is novel about these new ideologies is not only that they do not divide sharply the two political camps but that on the contrary, when linked to the means for bringing them about, they seem to elicit a wide margin of agreement. First, neither side has a clear formulation of how its vision of the society will be implemented; lack of clarity in formulating explicitly the means blurs the distinctiveness that the two camps profess. But even more, *specific* policy suggestions hardly differentiate the Left from the Center-Right. The political landscape looks very much like a football field where the two teams are expected to play a close game and where they will change sides every quarter!

Second, ideological propositions, according to all the surveys we have, interest only a part of the electorate—as little as 20 percent, certainly not more than 30 percent. The citizen's interests deal with everyday concrete issues, forcing the political parties in both camps to come up with specifics and in so doing to espouse common policies and solutions. For the French body politic consists of men and women who, as anywhere else, are interested in everyday practical problems—the cost of living, wages, social security, rents, employment and job security, old age protection in the form of medical care and retirement benefits, good schools and vacations. This is what we called the "nitty-gritty" of politics and on those issues both in the legislative and presidential elections the two camps were remarkably close. It is not then in terms of broad ideological aspirations and their success or failure that the future of the French society can be assessed, but rather in terms of the specifics. And in turn success or failure to provide specific policies will often be determined by circumstances. Much of the future of the French economy, for instance, and as a result the kind of society that will emerge, depends upon factors over which France does not have much control. A sharp rise in the price of oil, a rise in the price in some raw materials, the dislocation of the Common Market, the changing climate of the international relations will have far more important repercussions upon the French society than the choice of a President or his policies. In other words, it is very hard to speculate about future trends when the variables are unforeseeable.

Yet several internal problems must be spelled out. Broadly they relate to the political institutions and to the organization of the State in its relations to society, the future of the political parties and, finally, to the foreign policy of France with particular regard to the role and the position of France in the Common Market and its defense within or outside of the Atlantic Alliance.

The Political Institutions

The system remains more participatory than ever before. The people elect directly their President and are occasionally consulted on referendums. In case of conflict between President's government and the National Assembly, dissolution is likely to give the people a chance to decide. The political parties, by forming broad coalitional umbrellas, are seeking out votes with a mandate to form a government so that even in the legislative election the link between citizen and a government has been strengthened. As long as presidential dominance is based upon such a participation and involvement democratic government is guaranteed.

THE FUTURE OF PRESIDENTIALISM

The French form of presidentialism is about to be tested. Giscard d'Estaing does not have a strong party to rely upon. He has to rely upon the Gaullists (with about 185 deputies) and the centrists (110) and in so doing fashion a new safe presidential majority which cannot be "unconditional" and therefore must remain uncertain.

One direction the new President can follow in the name of a new presidential majority is to rely upon the Center and gradually whittle down the Gaullists to bring them under his own leadership and party label—whatever it may be. In such a case the new President will have to rely upon a new but equally docile "majority" in the National Assembly. The clearest indications of such a development will be resignations from the Gaullist party in support of the President's formation or a genuine combination of the centrists and the Gaullists under the President's instigation and leadership. In other words, we shall have a continuation of the Pompidou regime but without the Gaullist label. Coalition politics will continue.

There are other hypotheses to be considered. Giscard d'Estaing may move away from coalition politics directly into party politics, attempting to fashion out of the combination of the centrists and Gaullist forces a genuine party modelled after the British Conservatives, with organization, leadership and centralized control and of course mass membership. However, it seems that the same reasons that deterred Pompidou from moving in such a direction will influence the new President as well. He, too, wishes to stand over parties as the national spokesman; he, too, will fear that a tight party organization may overshadow him and limit his freedom of movement; he, too, will prefer to leave his "majority" fluid and open rather than transform it into a tight bloc that will repel newcomers and face the constant challenge of a well-organized oppositional bloc. But there are other reasons as well. Pompidou had a strong party behind him; it had, as we noted, an absolute majority in the National Assembly between 1968 to 1973. Giscard d'Estaing does not. To create one is far more difficult than it would have been for Pompidou. In addition, the centrist groups are too weak to act as a center of gravity. Besides, they will resist it. The character of the centrist parties has been lack of organization, discipline and mass membership. The Independent Republicans (an offshoot of the National Center of the Independents) do not have more than 20,000 members. They are truly a party of notables. To attempt to transform them into an organized and disciplined party that will swallow all the centrist groups and the Gaullists as well is a highly unlikely prospect. Finally, the only way for the new President to undermine the solidarity and the organization of the Left is to keep the door permanently open to some of its members, especially among some of the Socialists and the Radicals. A tight party formation under Giscard d'Estaing is likely to solidify the forces of the opposition at a time when the opposition needs just 1 percent of the votes to win.

Another hypothesis has been evoked by some political leaders and writers: a constitutional revision to provide for a genuine separation of powers between the presidency and the legislature. The right of dissolution by the President and correspondingly the right to censure and overthrow the government by the National Assembly would have to be abolished. The President will dispose of the totality of the executive power; the Parliament will have the last word on legislation without fear of being dissolved. The two branches of government will move on two different planes. The cabinet will become in law the President's cabinet and there will be no need for a Prime Minister. It is an intriguing hypothesis but unlikely to materialize.

The President will not be inclined to sponsor such constitutional reforms for fear of losing his influence and control over the National Assembly; the National Assembly itself will not accept it because it will be deprived of the constitutional powers through which it hopes to be able to control the Prime Minister and the President and thus to reassert its power. A separation of powers similar to the American system may prove unworkable. In the United States over a period of many years links between the Executive and Congress have been created to provide for many points of cooperation while legitimizing conflict and its resolution. The French system has not evolved any such links. An overt conflict between a presidential policy proposal and a legislative measure, for instance, will deadlock the system.

There is, however, the prospect of a modified version of the American system without constitutional reforms, without even a change in the electoral system. Coalition politics may break down and give place to a multiparty situation. In such a case there will be no presidential majority in the National Assembly and dissolution—while always an important threat—may not be effective in recreating a majority for the President. The President will have to deal on an ad hoc basis with the help of ad hoc majorities to enact his measures. The overthrow of his Prime Minister on a given policy measure will not be followed by dissolution but by an effort to find a new Prime Minister acceptable to a majority for a given set of policies. The President will have to compromise; the National Assembly will recover some of its influence and legislative powers. But the basis of presidentialism will remain and so will the prospects for the President of refashioning at some time a presidential majority. The system will be more flexible and adjustable to circumstances and political trends. The President himself, freed from the obligations to a given presidential majority, may strike out through a given Prime Minister for policies he would not have dared to envisage if he had to rely upon the same presidential majority. Multipartism and presidentialism may in fact strengthen both the presidency and the National Assembly in their respective roles of policy-initiation and legislation. Cabinet instability will not have the same debilitating impact it had under the Fourth Republic by undermining, as it did, executive leadership. On the contrary, it will become a flexible mechanism under the President for policy-making. Successive Prime Ministers and cabinets for limited periods of time and for specific policy goals under the overall direction of the President may provide for such a flexible means of policy-making.

There is finally the prospect of diminished presidential power and a reassertion of parliamentary supremacy. As we noted, it may occur only if a solid, well organized majority in the National Assembly is opposed to the President. But the defenses available to the President in such a case are impressive. He has broad ordinance power to legislate in fact by decree in a number of areas thus bypassing the National Assembly; he can call for referendums; he can, above all, manipulate the opposition by changing his Prime Minister; he can ultimately dissolve and call for an election. But if these defenses seem impressive, they have an Achilles' heel. The opposition to the President may win a legislative election; then the President cannot dissolve again and call for a new election for a year. It is this possibility—which every President is likely to avoid—that constitutes the major pitfall for the French presidency. For if this possibility were to materialize then inevitably a Prime Minister opposed to him would emerge as the leader of the new majority. A deadlock between the two branches is likely to develop—a deadlock, however, that is likely to be to the advantage of the National Assembly. In the last analysis the President will have to submit or to resign. The Prime Minister will gradually emerge as the political leader and the presidency will be overshadowed. The pendulum will swing from the Executive to the legislature.

But even such a possibility, so often evoked by many French constitutional writers, may amount only to a transfer of the powers of the President to that of the Prime Minister, *as long as the latter is the leader of a solid and coherent majority.* The presidential prerogatives, even the personal ones, will be used by the Prime Minister. Executive leadership under a Prime Minister supported by a majority will replace presidentialism. Parliamentary government will be restored. In other words, the only condition that can overshadow the President—a strong united and coherent majority *against* him—will provide for the strength and the support a Prime Minister will need to exercise executive leadership. There will be no return to a government by the Assembly, as under the Fourth Republic.

PRESIDENTIALISM UNDER GISCARD D' ESTAING

As soon as the election results were announced, no doubt was left that Giscard d'Estaing planned to emphasize presidential leadership. He set up broad policy directives and even announced specific and detailed policy measures: the rise in the minimum wages and retirement benefits, the declaration that France would again offer asylum to political exiles, the suppression of wiretapping, and an end to the sale of arms to regimes that do not pursue "liberal" policies. Without a cabinet meeting he ordered continuing the nuclear tests and when one of the newly appointed Ministers protested, the President removed him from office.

Forming the cabinet was also a presidential matter and he left no doubt in anybody's mind that not only the Prime Minister but every cabinet officer derived their authority from the President. The new President broke precedent by appearing before television to announce and explain the composition of his cabinet, the qualifications of each one of his Ministers and introduce them to the public. Subsequently in a message to Parliament he spelled out the policies he envisaged and indicated that the Prime Minister would present them in greater detail to the National Assembly. He added that he had authorized the Prime Minister to ask for a vote of confidence on his programmatic declaration.

The Cabinet

The organization of the cabinet appointed by the new President was an expression of significant administrative and political changes. The cabinet consists of a total of thirty-six members and is one of the largest ever in the Fifth Republic. However, only fifteen have Ministerial posts forming a small group that deliberates on policy issues. The others, twenty-one in all, are Secretaries of State attached to the Prime Minister or to a Ministry or with an autonomous status. In this manner, the President expects to use the hard core of the cabinet for consultations and deliberations, leaving to the Secretaries of State the role of implementation and execution.

Several new cabinet posts were created. The Ministry of Reforms was charged with advanced planning for the future. (The first incumbent lasted only thirteen days and was dismissed when he sharply criticized the French nuclear tests.) A Ministry for the Quality of Life was also established. Among the Secretaries of State, a number of innovations indicate the same concern with social problems. There are special posts for Universities, for professional education and for adult education, for penitentiaries, for the foreign workers in France, and for social policies that directly affect women.

Equally noticeable was the political turnover of personnel. Of the thirty-six cabinet members only nine belonged to the previous government, and only two maintained the same positions. Six of the newcomers came from the Ecole Nationale d'Administration; three studied in the Institute of Political Studies and four had held civil service posts. The average age is about fifty, but many important posts, including that of the Prime Minister, were occupied by men in their early forties. Three women were in the cabinet—two with a Ministerial position and the third as a Secretary of State. This is not enough, but it is a beginning toward fulfilling electoral promises.

From a political point of view the cabinet turnover amounted to what many called the "destruction of the Gaullist State," an allusion to the tight control the Gaullists had exercised over the cabinet. The Gaullists received a total of five Ministries and seven Secretariats of State—just one-third. The Independent Republicans with not more than fifty-five deputies—about a sixth of the new majority—received seven. The CDP, which had supported on the first ballot Chaban-Delmas, got only two Secretariats, perhaps not more than they deserved since their group amounts to less than thirty deputies. In contrast, the *Réformateurs* who moved out of their opposition to support Giscard d'Estaing, received a total of three Ministries and three secretariats, though they do not account for more than thirty-four deputies in the National Assembly.

The imbalance becomes even more pronounced when we compare the political composition of the new cabinet with previous ones under Pompidou. In virtually all of them the Gaullists held 60 to 70 percent of all posts; they were reduced to one-third. Obviously the new President was organizing his new cabinet with an eye to the support he could receive from the centrists, as well as to put the Gaullists on a good behavior notice. Additional ministerial posts might be made available to them depending on their behavior in the National Assembly and on their willingness to support him and cooperate. There was also a hint that those who did so and abandoned the Gaullist party might be rewarded.

A final observation: the cabinet included more nonparliamentarians than any cabinet under Pompidou. Now there are ten—more than 25 percent of the total. They included the Minister of Foreign Affairs, the Minister of Health, the Minister of Reforms, the Minister of Education, and six Secretaries of State. The Prime Minister submitted the government's program to the National Assembly and received its approval with 297 votes in favor and 181 against with a handful of abstentions. The "new" presidential majority stood firmly behind him and in the debates that followed supported the Prime Minister. There was no question of a defection though their support of the Gaullists, it was stated, was "conditional."

The cabinet is to meet once a week under the direction of the President to discuss general policy issues. But the major decisions will emanate from the President to be implemented by the Prime Minister and the individual Ministers involved. "Small" cabinet meetings, consisting of the President and one or two Ministers, work out *together* the measures to be announced, the decrees to be issued, or the bills to be submitted to the National Assembly. But the cabinet is likely to play only a limited role in the presidential decisions. The President continues to be assisted by a staff of experts, mostly civil servants, who can reach out, as in the past, into individual Ministries to dictate the presidential point of view. They interact with the administrative staffs of the Prime Minister and the other Ministers. A hard core of some 250 to 300 expert administrators comprise the office of the presidency and the staffs of the Ministers. There are at least about 200 more in nationalized and public services and in the Planning Commission, forming a total of about 500 that play a crucial role in policy preparation, deliberation and decision-making. In addition, about 100 officers of the Treasury (the Ministry of Finance) play a key role either directly or indirectly (by virtue of their assignment to individual Ministries) in scrutinizing and passing on projected expenditures by all the various governmental agencies and the Ministries. Perhaps as many as another 150 are placed in the so-called "horizontal administration,"—that is, in key committees to arbitrate between conflicting administrative demands. Under the dominance of the new President the "administrative state" appears as powerful as in the past.

The Legislature

As with his predecessor, Giscard d'Estaing expressed his firm resolution to open up the dialogue with the legislative branch, to give them more freedom in proposing and scrutinizing legislation and in controlling the cabinet. He asserted his firm belief that a government was obliged to give its place to a new one when it lost support. In an effort to please the Senate he appointed a Senator in his cabinet and, as noted, to show his deference to the National Assembly, he asked his Prime Minister to ask for a vote on his programmatic declaration. But he also suggested two important reforms calculated to increase the powers of the legislature or at least to strengthen its influence. First, without going as far as some had suggested to establish a special status for "the opposition" (as is the case in Great Britain) he nonetheless undertook the obligation to consult with its leaders on important national issues, especially defense and foreign policy matters. Second, he urged the National Assembly to change its by-laws and allow both "the opposition" and "the majority" in the National Assembly to ask questions on urgent and important national matters once a week. The Prime Minister and the cabinet members have been requested by the President to be present to answer such questions.

Finally, in the course of a debate on an important government bill, when a number of amendments were introduced that went far beyond its original scope, the Minister of Justice speaking on behalf of the government assured everybody that he would not ask for a "blocked vote" (requesting the Assembly to rule out all amendments and vote on the original bill). The new Minister, a former member of the opposition, said that he had been the victim of the "blocked vote" too often to use it again. Was this a hint that the government would refrain from using it, thus strengthening the legislative power of the Assembly and its committees? In a rare display of political courage the President also urged lowering the voting age to eighteen. The National Assembly and the Senate enacted it and also decreed that eighteen-year olds be given full civil responsibility. Now they can marry, divorce, open a bank account, be liable for their acts, and so forth.

Constitutional Reforms

Since 1958 the Gaullist Constitution has remained intact. Minor changes were made regarding the timing of the parliamentary sessions, the independence of the former members of the French Community (mostly the colonies in French-speaking Africa), and of course the granting of Algerian independence. The only major reform—the direct election of the President by universal direct popular franchise—was proposed by DeGaulle himself in 1962 and adopted by the people in a referendum. It is an integral part of the "Gaullist constitution." Pompidou, as we have seen, proposed to reduce the President's term of office from seven to five years but was forced to withdraw his project, which many of the Gaullists had opposed. In fact, the Gaullists became increasingly fundamentalist on matters of constitutional reform; they saw in the Constitution the most tangible element of the Gaullist legacy and cautioned against any "fooling around with it."

The new President in his first message to Parliament suggested a series of reforms, most of which had been advocated also by the Left. He did not mention reducing the presidential term, which he favors. But he proceeded to outline the following: changing the present constitutional provision according to which a deputy resigns his seat if he becomes a cabinet member to be replaced by his "substitute" whose name appeared with his on the ballot at election time. In the last years constant, even if minor, reshufflings of the cabinets had gradually eliminated several elected deputies. In 1974 it was estimated that over sixty "substitutes" sat in the National Assembly, while the elected deputies who had become Ministers and then were dismissed or resigned found themselves without a political role. The proposal will allow a deputy who accepted a cabinet post to return to his parliamentary seat six months after he ceases to be a Minister. This would make it possible for many Gaullist Ministers who are no longer in the cabinet to return to the National Assembly.

Second, the ease with which candidates for the presidency were "designated" accounted for their proliferation. Many of them were not serious candidates, and wished only to avail themselves of radio and TV time. The proposed revision will tighten the conditions of nomination. Thus the media—both radio and television—will be made available only to a few and serious challengers. The presidential election will be given the seriousness and solemnity it deserves.

The President of the Republic suggested also modifying the jurisdiction of the Constitutional Council. The Council was set up originally to arbitrate conflicts between the Executive and the legislature; in fact, to protect the Executive against legislative encroachments. The suggested reforms imply an evolution of the Council in the direction of the U.S. Supreme Court. It will examine on its own initiative any case involving a derogation of individual rights. However, individuals will not be allowed to bring directly a case before the Council. Only the President of the Republic, the Prime Minister, the President of the National Assembly and the President of the Senate can bring a complaint before it according to the present Constitution. The reform envisages giving the same power to any forty members of Parliament.

THE POLITICAL FORCES: FRAGMENTATION VS. COALITION

We have seen that both in the legislative election of March 1973 and in the presidential election of May 1974 the accent was on coalition politics. Both on the Left and on the Right or Center-Right large formations, comprising smaller parties, faced each other. There was no question about a two-party system but rather of the bipolarization of the political forces into two coalitional blocs. There was a "presidential majority" in 1965, a "new presidential majority" in 1969, and a "new enlarged presidential majority" in 1974, stretching from the Gaullists to the *Réformateurs*. There was an "opposition" (the Union of the Left) stretching from the left-wing Radical Socialist to the Extreme Left. Within each coalition there were smaller ones. For instance, the Socialists and left-wing Radicals joined forces in the legislative election; the *Réformateurs* included at least four small formations; finally, the URP included three formations: the CDP, the Independent Republicans and the Gaullists. They formed the "majority coalition" to which the *Réformateurs* were added in the presidential "majority" of 1974.

The key problem about the future of French politics is the viability of these coalitions as opposed to the only other realistic alternative— fragmentation. For the prospect of two unified and centralized political parties is highly unlikely. Much will depend on the tactics of the new President, the attitude of the Gaullist party, and the continuation of the Communist–Socialist alliance. But a great deal will also depend upon episodic and adventitious factors, some of which may solidify the coalitions and others cause their disintegration. It is impossible to predict. It is only possible to identify the trends that have been noticeable ever since the death of Pompidou and the new presidential election.

Both trends—solidarity and disintegration—are noticeable. To the Left the movement in the direction of unity appears strong. The Socialist party, in cooperation with the leader of one Trade Union organization—the CFDT (French Confederation of Democratic Labor) with a membership of about 700,000—decided to convene all the Socialist groups and organize themselves into one movement. It may result in a confederation that will include a number of splinter Socialist and leftist groups and a number of isolated political leaders, including even some left-wing Gaullists who opted for Mitterrand. In this manner the internal splits among the Socialists will come to an end; the new Socialist movement will boost its membership, (already the Socialist party claims now over 100,000 members). It will also increase its voting strength and be in a position to dislodge the Communists from their position as the "first party of the Left." It will attract intellectuals and students and appeal to many centrist and Gaullist voters. François Mitterrand, fresh from his remarkably strong vote in the presidential election, has assumed the leadership of this undertaking while pledging fully close cooperation with the Communist party.

A new broader Socialist coalition allied with the Communists for electoral purposes may well develop. Two qualifications must be made, however. The left-wing Radicals are reluctant to become an integral part of it. They wish to revive their independent and autonomous party in association with the Left. They, too, have hopes of attracting independent political leaders, some from among the Gaullists. To the left of the Socialist "family" itself there are two groups that may prove recalcitrant. The PSU has already declared that it will not join a Socialist formation at the expense of its own independence and identity. But another Socialist group—the so-called CERES *(Centre d'Etudes et des Recherches de l'Education Socialiste)* committed to "guild-socialism"—has developed into a faction. The Communist party, despite its profession of cooperation, has no interests in seeing all the Socialists and the left-wing Radicals unite to become a stronger party. They will do everything in their power to encourage the left-wing Radicals and the left-wing splinters to maintain their autonomy and independence. Thus the unity of the Left attained in 1973 and reaffirmed in the presidential election of 1974 remains precarious.

The situation in the center is far more fluid. At least five centrist groups seek to form some kind of broad coalition. The *Réformateurs* are a small coalition consisting of the Centrist Union and the Radicals that supported Giscard d'Estaing but also of two other splinters: the Republican Union and the Democratic-Socialist party and some old-time Independents with grassroot support but no political organization. The

CDP consists of the centrists who supported Pompidou and who also rallied to Giscard d'Estaing on the second ballot. Finally, the President's party—the Independent Republicans—has been a part of "the majority" in alliance with the Gaullists since 1962. All of them together have kept alive the centrist vocation. Together they represented at least 25 percent of the votes in the legislative election of 1973. With Giscard d'Estaing as president and the defeat of the Gaullists, their electoral strength may well exceed that of the latter. But will they be able to unite? And if they do under what form? Will they reach out into the Gaullist ranks and if so what will be the reaction of the Gaullists?

It is impossible to answer these questions. Efforts have begun to fashion unity. One of the leaders of the Independent Republicans has already called for the formation of a "vast movement that is both social and liberal." The leader of the Centrist Union, Jean Lecanuet, however, has refused to allow his party to be absorbed by such a movement. The centrist leader favors the fusion of the Centrist Union with the CDP. Nothing separates them any more after joining forces to support the same President and to participate in his cabinet. One of the leaders of the Independent Republicans has broadened the scope of a coalition to support the President by stretching his hand to "his Gaullist friends" but also to many Socialists for whom close association with the Communists is undesirable. His goal is a genuine centrist federation to include all the centrist groups and to bite into the strength of the Socialists, Radical Socialists and Gaullists. It will be a federation committed to supporting the new President whose electoral strength will be quickly tested both in the forthcoming senatorial elections and in many by-elections for the National Assembly. It is a federation whose strength is predicated on the development of grassroot support and departmental and regional implantation and organization—through individual and discrete contacts and arrangements rather than the formation of a mass party. Already, important administrative changes of departmental and regional officials—a turnover of about 30 percent since Giscard d'Estaing became President—indicate that the plan is being put into operation.

And what about the Gaullists? One might have expected that defeat would have consolidated their discipline. Yet lack of leadership and losing the presidency for the first time has demoralized and divided them. The fragmentation that we noted in the last year of Pompidou's presidency has continued. Three different tendencies within the Party are apparent. One is in accord with the hopes of the centrists: the so-called *New Social Contract,* headed by a Prime Minister of the Fourth Republic and now Speaker of the National Assembly—Edgar Faure— is a "study" group comprising over eighty deputies. More than half come from the Gaullists and the others come from among the centrists and *Réformateurs*. It constitutes the wedge that may be driven into the body of the Gaullists to bring converts into the hands of the centrists and the Independent Republicans to form a truly centrist majority for the new President. The second trend is gradual fragmentation: two Gaullist leaders have already urged the formation of a new party to carry on the social doctrine of Gaullism. The young Gaullists of the Progressive Front have called for a participation in the new Socialist movement. The former Minister of Foreign Affairs, Michel Jobert, has also struck out on his own in the name of the Gaullist heritage of national independence and social reform. So have some others. Finally, many of the Gaullist traditional leaders, including the Gaullist official newspaper, argue for the withdrawal of the Gaullist party—the UDR—from the "majority coalition" so that the party can refashion its organization and above all elect a leader.

Faced with the prospect of the conversion of forty or fifty deputies to the centrist presidential formation, the emergence of splinter groups, and the prospect of a direct confrontation between some of the Gaullist traditional leaders and the new President—the Gaullists are going through difficult times. The safest course for the Gaullist parliamentarians is to remain within the "majority" and support the new President until election time. But what is safest for them amounts in effect to the erosion of the party, the loss of its identity, and ultimately to the inevitable conversion of many to the new presidential majority under the direction of the centrists. Time will bring about defections, new dissensions, the weakening of their departmental organization, and the loss of membership. The only alternative is to join forces with the Left and vote against the President's government to be forced, as a result, into a new election whose prospect is grim. As a French political leader put it, faced with the choice of being raped or committing suicide they are likely to opt for the first!

In the last analysis, however, the evolution of the political forces may depend on adventitious circumstances. The trend toward coalitional formations has its own momentum and so does the opposite trend towards fragmentation. If the Left remains united, it will force the centrists and the Gaullists to stay together. If the Left divides, then it is quite likely that the Center and the Gaullists will divide internally and separate from each other. The role of the President is of capital importance. He and his lieutenants may in the course of time fashion a genuine centrist coalition that will inevitably include many of the Gaullists. If he fails he may suggest and support a new electoral law leaning toward proportional representation, especially if he realizes that he not only doesn't have a majority, but that he is about to be faced by a negative one (Gaullists and the Left). Thus he will accelerate a fragmentation to avoid a hostile majority. Such an electoral reform will be supported by all parliamentary groups other than the Gaullists. The Left advocated it and so did many centrists. Or the President may threaten dissolution to keep his present "majority" under control. Finally, he may resign himself, as we have intimated, to a fragmented National Assembly and to ad hoc majorities with different Prime Ministers and cabinets for different policies. Thus he is likely to play a key role in the evolution of political forces as they go through a crucial period of change whose extremes are either the formation of two coalitions—the Left vs. "presidential majority"—or a fragmentation that will resurrect multipartism.

Foreign Policy: In Search of a Role

The year 1973 was for President Pompidou similar to what 1968 had been for General DeGaulle. There were many indications of France's weakness and its inability to play a role in the Mediterranean and Europe: the oil crisis, the war in the Mideast, the negotiations between the two super powers to put an end to the war there without the participation of "Europe," and the strong line taken by Henry Kissinger and President Nixon urging the Common Market countries not to make decisions without prior consultations with the United States. Also, there were the internal conflicts within the Common Market and the decisions of individual countries, including France itself, to abandon a common monetary policy and to invoke special measures to protect their economies. It was perhaps this realization that led the dying President and his Foreign Minister to return to the Gaullist hard line of national independence against the United States and to a belated search for a "European identity," and a "European defense."

But France's partners in the Common Market were unwilling to follow French leadership. In Britain, the election of a Labour Government on February 28, 1974, committed to renegotiating the terms of Britain's entry into the Common Market and the added economic difficulties caused by mounting inflation seem to presage the dislocation of the Common Market, not only as a political entity, which as we have seen it was never allowed to become, but also as an economic one.

Like Pompidou, Giscard d'Estaing ran in the presidential election as a "European." But unlike Pompidou, he seems inclined to follow a different approach to the reconstruction of Europe. First and foremost he seems to be returning to DeGaulle's realization that only through a firm consolidation of the relationship between France and West Germany can a European vocation be kept alive and prosper. The first political leader to visit him in June 1974 was his former fellow Minister of Finance of West Germany and now Chancellor, Kurt Schmidt, and he returned the visit within a few weeks. The new Minister of Foreign Affairs was the former French Ambassador to West Germany; he was appointed because of the great importance the new President attributed to Franco-German relations.

There is every indication that European unity will not be pursued though grandiose Summit meetings, as with Pompidou, but in terms of careful and painstaking deliberations between heads of state, and in the Council of Ministers and in the Executive Commission of the Common Market countries. The "two-track" Europe seems to be in the process of being abandoned in favor of ad hoc arrangements in which the Council of Ministers and the Commission work together on both political and economic matters. The sharp distinction between what is "political" (to be decided by the heads of states outside the Common Market institutions and without consultations with the Commission) and what is "economic" (to be decided in consultation with the Common Market organizations)—a distinction so forcefully made in the past by the French—may be abandoned.

In the declaration of the NATO countries in Ottawa and subsequently in Brussels in the summer of 1974 the "identity" of Europe was recognized and so was its freedom to act and to negotiate with others without any binding obligation to prior consultations with her Atlantic partners—notably the United States. But such consultations were deemed to be "necessary" and "highly desirable." Thus the declaration on "European independence" sought by the Gaullists in the past and especially by Pompidou's Foreign Minister gave place to an assertion of an "identity" of Europe *in* the context of the realities of the Atlantic Alliance.

Similarly in matters of defense the disagreements between France and virtually every other member of the Alliance are being reconciled. There is no question any longer of an "independent defense," as the French insisted, but of the "distinct" defense problems of Western Europe, their "specificity" and recognition of the contribution of the European (that is, French and British) nuclear deterrence to the Atlantic defense. The General Chief of Staff, General François Maurin, continued to argue in favor of a French national nuclear striking force but he conceded that it was the duty of France to foresee all possibilities, and if France were to engage in battle ". . . in the framework of the Alliance," to determine and define in advance the procedures in terms of which France will engage its forces. "Consultations for this purpose are going on with the appropriate NATO organs," he added.[1] This appears to be another step toward closer cooperation with NATO. Though the word integration is avoided, it eliminates one of the most serious weaknesses in the strategy of France as it had developed under DeGaulle and Pompidou.

There is every indication that France is returning to the realities of the international situation in realizing that its new role is above all in Europe but within the framework of the Atlantic Alliance. The presence of American forces in Europe, the support for such forces (the NATO declaration specifies the need for substantial American forces not only "presently" but for the future) was explicitly accepted. The argument in favor of a separate and independent European defense, ultimately without the United States and the Atlantic Alliance and without close consultations with the United States, seems to have given place to the realistic demands of the other European countries in favor of both European cooperation *and* consultations with the United States in the framework of the Alliance. The use of terms such as the "specificity" and the "identity" and the "individual" European nuclear contribution to the Alliance satisfies the French. They have conceded, however, to their European allies the need for cooperation and consultation and of close relations with NATO (i.e., with the United States) in the development of an overall European defense strategy.

A critical indication of France's attitude in the development of a European common defense will be its participation in the so-called "Euro-Group"—the organization consisting of all European countries members of NATO (except France, Iceland and Portugal) for standardizing armaments within the framework of NATO. Both its strong NATO attachment and the fear that such standardization would lead to American domination had kept the French out. Strong incentives—other than the overall commitment to the "specificity" of the European defense—may lead France to reconsider. One such incentive is the prospect of finding clients for their aeronautical industry. The European forces will have to be re-equipped with fighter planes and the French Mirages IV are likely to be sought by Belgium and other Western allies on condition, however, that France enter into the Euro-Group and accept both the logic of armaments standardization and NATO cooperation. A similarly important indication will be France's willingness to join with other Common Market countries in producing enrichened uranium.

But the problems of a political European Union—which was not mentioned as such—are far from being solved. The new President stated that he would live up to the timetable set at the Summit of Paris to establish such a European Union by 1980. The British are reluctant and the economic problems facing individual countries and the Common Market as a whole are likely to have precedence over any ambitious political decisions. But as with economic arrangements in the past, there is for the first time a realization of the need for a joint foreign policy for the Nine. Ad hoc arrangements and consultations among the Nine with the participation of the European Commission are more likely to

lead to a political Europe than a solemn drafting of a political confeder-
ational charter or the election of a European Parliament directly by the
peoples. It is true that the veto power of each individual state and
especially of France continues to be the overriding reality in all such
consultative arrangements. Yet the very fact that the effort is being
made to have the Nine agree and "speak with one voice" will inevitably
lead—barring major political and economic crises—to more binding
institutional arrangements. As it was with the economic Europe a political one, if at all made, is likely to be made gradually, step by step, and
only when the need for unity is clearly perceived by the political leaders
of the Nine. For the first time the French political leadership seems
committed to making this effort not to establish French supremacy but
in a truly cooperative spirit that calls for reciprocity and concessions by
all.

   While Europe and the relations between the Nine and the United
States constitute the most important foreign policy issue for France, its
commitment to French-speaking Africa in terms of its existing economic, cultural and military arrangements has been reasserted. Thus a
full Ministerial post, the Ministry of Cooperation, was established to
deal with French-speaking Africa and Madagascar and sub-Sahara
Africa. Also, a more conciliatory attitude toward Israel is apparent. The
Minister of Foreign Affairs promised to visit Israel in an effort to improve relations there and with the whole Eastern Mediterranean world.

   In summary, the new foreign policy of the new President may well
put an end to France's isolation in Europe or in the Atlantic Alliance and
also in the Mediterranean. Economic and industrial cooperation will be
as actively pursued as in the past. Already agreements in the area of
nuclear energy and industrial development between Iran and France
may provide a basis of a cooperation there. Above all, France may seek
a new role as a member of the European Community and *in* the European Community in *close* cooperation with West Germany. It will
improve its relations with NATO in matters of strategy and defense.
The ambitious and grandiose projects to become a "balancer" between
East and West; to undermine the position of the United States or the
Soviet Union; to create an independent Europe under French leadership,
and to provide for a credible nuclear deterrent outside of the Atlantic
Alliance—propounded by DeGaulle and occasionally nourished by
Pompidou, especially in his last year in office—are no longer seriously
entertained. The nostalgia for the glories of the past has given place to
realizing the opportunities of the present. France and Western Europe
have a role to play in Africa, in the Mediterranean and in the European
continent through an Atlantic cooperation that can ultimately lead to
genuine strength and independence.

How to "Unblock" the Society[2]

Chaban-Delmas' vision of a New Society was based on a strong indictment of an all-encompassing State. It does not allow for genuine local autonomy; it prevents cultural pluralism; it inhibits differentiation of activities and pursuits in regions, towns and municipalities; it prevents a vigorous associational participatory activity in culture, in politics, and in work, as well as in the development of individual entrepreneurship. It "blocks" the French men and women from becoming free to shape their lives and destinies in the various roles they perform. It thwarts spontaneity; it prevents the individual from becoming a full citizen.

There seems to be widespread agreement that the French society remained blocked. The State continues to have the monopoly of "initiative" and reform. The individuals, while they constantly contest and occasionally defy the State, expect it at the same time to provide for reform and solutions to all social problems. Professor Crozier attributes the blocked society to centralization and stratification, to the stifling of local and associational initiative and to the lack of communication among social groups, notably between the administration and those administered. It is a rational and efficient state system but in a rapidly developing and modernizing society it becomes increasingly anachronistic. Professor Hoffmann, who follows the analysis of Crozier, writes:

> In a nation riddled by conflicts, the citizens have traditionally preferred to entrust the solution of conflicts to higher authority. . . . But authoritarianism has always been tempered by individualism, by the citizen's determination to be protected from arbitrariness through a network of bureaucratic rules limiting the scope and intensity of authority. France is thus marked by a series of polar opposites: rigid, often stifling regulations, but also the preservation of the individual's capacity to protest . . .; tight hierarchies controlled by a handful of important people, but also the fulfillment of the small peoples' dream of legal equality; centralization, but also fragmentation into small groups and castes; official, hierarchical relations, but also informal "parallel" relations that often find the formal superiors depending on their subordinates. Liberty is freedom *from*, not freedom *to;* it is defined as resistance and nondependence; compromise is a pejorative word. . . . In a system like this, the pattern of change is unique: the *way* of change is cataclysmic, not gradual; the nonparticipating citizens, when dissatisfied, behave not like reformers, but like rebels, given to wild utopianism, intransigence, and self-righteousness. . . .
>
> . . . The new demand for participation, incoherent and inchoate as it may be, shows that the French feel the increasing irrelevance of their old style.[3]

Similarly, but somewhat with greater caution, Philip Williams and Martin Harrison write, "The French conceive of authority as absolute, anonymous and monarchic, yet egalitarian. This conception inhibits initiative and imagination at the lower levels, produces impersonality, suspicion and unhelpfulness in relations with the public, and can turn simple administrative transactions into a nightmare of form filling and frustration."[4] An interesting illustration of this was recently given in a newspaper article indicating that twenty-two separate formal administrative acts were needed to decide to build a secondary high school, requiring the concurrence of fourteen district administrators.[5]

While much in this overall analysis may be true, it seems to be unduly critical of the French administration and of the organization of the state. It reflects judgments that are inspired by the American model of liberalism that emphasizes associational and group activity that reduces the state and the administrative machinery to a mere reflection of the well-organized competing societal groups and forces. Yet such a model can be just as inefficient when it comes to policy-making. While it lacks the stifling character of an all-encompassing administrative machinery and stresses participation and grassroots initiative, it may produce a chronic stalemate because the relative equal weight of competing groups may offset each other to produce no policy at all. The society—free and spontaneous—may become stalemated and blocked. The thesis presented is also unduly critical of what the French administration has accomplished in the last generation and under the Gaullist regime. Lastly, it doesn't do justice to the fact that the very achievements of the French administration may have created the condition for reform. There is no doubt that the Gaullist legacy and many of the Gaullist leaders, in seeing in the State the expression of the society, the embodiment of its needs and aspirations and the initiator of change, have perpetuated and enhanced the State's dominance and control over all areas of social life. But is is equally true that the rapid industrialization and prosperity the country experienced have released forces that run counter to state centralization and control. For example, it is easier for a state to "control" the universities if there are 150,000 students and a corresponding small number of professors. It is far more difficult to do so when the students reach 700,000 and the number of professors are counted in the tens of thousands. At the secondary education level, the task becomes impossible when the number of students reaches into the millions. Similarly, when industrial firms are encouraged to merge and grow to become powerful competitive units within the Common Market they begin to have more influence with the State, and often against the State, than small dispersed firms. Also, when nationalized services and public services begin to serve millions of consumers there is inevitably a need to grant them discretion and autonomy and a degree of initiative and experimentation in adjusting service to needs. In other words, sheer quantitative changes makes statism as an administrative phenomenon difficult—perhaps even too expensive. Within the Gaullist State, centralized and hierarchical, with a great reliance upon top experts and administrators, the very seeds of an opening were planted. The Leviathan begins to have hollow feet.

We may be reaching the time where the French polity, while continuing to rely upon strong administrative guidance, will give greater freedom to local and associational initiative. This is the problem of administrative reform. We may also be reaching a point where stratification and fragmentation is giving place to communication. This can be accomplished in part through educational and in part through administrative reform. We may be reaching a stage where the monopoly of the State in matters of information may well lead to a more pluralistic development. This is the problem, at least in part, of reorganizing the Radio and Television services in the nation. We are reaching also a point where the younger people may feel more at home with their political institutions. This is already partly accomplished through lowering the voting age and granting full adulthood to all those who are 18. We are also rapidly reaching a point where the women may at long last reach equality with men; the first act of the new government and the Assembly not only provided for sexual education and information but allowed women (even minors) to use whatever contraceptives they wish—including the pill—if their physician prescribes them. What is more, the harsh "administrative state" pays for all such expenses!

We are also reaching a stage where group and voluntary activity in France is just as pervasive and intense as in any modern society. The farmers, the artisans, the workers, the veterans, the Algerian refugees, hundreds of lay Catholic organizations, the civil servants themselves, parapolitical groups like the political clubs, the students, PTA groups, the merchants and shopkeepers, local elected officials, environmentalists, and so forth: all are actively defending their interests not *against* the State or *through* the State, but also *in partnership* with the State. Even the reform of the industrial firm is beginning by providing a degree of participation of all its members in deciding what to produce and how to organize internally its activities. Participation is in the air!

THE PRECONDITIONS OF A PARTICIPATORY POLITY

There are certain minimal preconditions for the development of political participation. They constitute what we might call here the "take-off" stage. They are mostly economic and quantitative in nature. Under both DeGaulle and President Pompidou the "industrial phenomenon" had been as important as what Crozier has called the "bureaucratic phenomenon." The population has grown and if we include the foreign workers and their families it will undoubtedly reach 57 million by 1980. With regard to gross national product and per capita income, France has surpassed England and is beginning to vie with Germany. According to some, it will be the first European industrial power by 1980–1985. Its active population—static for about fifteen years (just about 20 million)—will increase rapidly after 1980 when the older groups disappear and the bulging group that is now below twenty-one moves into the market. Urbanization is moving fast, creating for the first time meaningful and separate urban centers with distinct and discrete problems and policy solutions. The educational opportunities have increased faster than anywhere else in Europe (with the possible exception of Sweden). The public sector—involving the production of electricity, gas, transportation, nuclear energy, automobiles (in part), coal, highways construction, as well as the role of the State in economic planning, has imposed administrative burdens that can hardly be tackled on the basis of a single administrative formula or on the basis of centralized decision-making. Economic planning, the development of nuclear energy, the expansion of the educational apparatus and facilities, the European economic integration, the rapid relocation of some 1,000,000 French refugees from Algeria, even—and this is a contested point—the impulse given to the private sector of the economy towards concentration of firms and receptivity to foreign (U.S.) investments—all have been the result of administrative initiative. Added to them is an impressive social legislation policy—virtually full coverage for medical care; four weeks paid vacations; rental subsidies, generous family support for children; free education and perhaps less generous but nonetheless fairly advanced when it comes to minimum wages, old age pension. All these changes have been due to the initiatives of the administrative state—the "blocked society." They have created the conditions of reform.

THE AGE OF REFORM

Both in the legislative election of 1973 and in the presidential election of 1974, the major and common theme of the two competing coalitions and candidates was reform: structural reforms; gradual reforms within the status quo; qualitative reforms dealing with the conditions of life and the goals of the industrial society. The call for reform is only a manifestation of the need for changes to adapt the political institutions to the realities and the needs of the society. General De-Gaulle himself in proposing in 1969 to reform the administrative state toward decentralization and pluralism called for changes that would give "to each one, in his place of work" the possibilities to participate actively in shaping his or her destiny instead of being "a passive instrument." He called it "the great French reform of the century."[6] The first Prime Minister under Pompidou, Chaban-Delmas, called a few months later for a new participatory society. The proposed reforms, however, were not carried out. There was a period of waiting. Reforms are now again before the new President, and his policies will determine the nature of the modernization—at long last—of the French State.

Administrative Reform

The future of what continues to be the Napoleonic structure of the French administrative system based upon centralization and hierarchical organization is at stake. The central decision-making organ is the "government" in Paris. Subordinate officials in each of the 95 Departments—the *préfets*—implement the decisions of the central government assisted by departmental councils. Some 35,000 mayors, elected by the municipal councils, also represent the national government and operate under the tutelage of the *préfet*. In addition to centralization and hierarchy, the system provided for symmetry: decisions made from the top are applied, with some exceptions for Alsace and Lorraine, uniformly throughout the country. Education, social security, minimum wages, sanitary rules, penitentiaries, the opening and closing of museums—all are decided at the top.

This neat organizational model began to break down. First, the *préfet* as the agent of the central government began to be superseded by other administrative officials of the central government delegated to implement national policies at the departmental level. Questions of urban and regional development, relocation of firms, the supervision of educational policies, allocation of resources, planning decisions as they applied to various parts of the country were implemented directly by the government through its agents without the intervention of the *préfet*. Second, the *préfet* was superseded—at least in law—by the formation of "regions" (twenty-two in all). These regions grouped together a number of departments already too small to constitute separate units for administrative and policy-making purposes. But the powers of the *"préfet* of the region" remained ambiguous and his position was never made strong; the end result was a greater degree of centralization since the powers taken away from the *préfet* were carried out directly by the national government through its agents or the regional *préfet*. In 1964 an administrative reform, curiously enough in the name of decentralization, returned to the traditional pattern by making once more the departmental *préfet* responsible for implementing national policy in his department by putting all agents of the national government under his jurisdiction.

At this juncture the demand for genuine decentralization and participation became more vocal than ever. Decentralization meant in essence delegating decision-making functions to subordinate departmental, regional, urban, or local units. A greater room for local initiative was thus to be allowed, while the "commanding heights" of state action —control over resources and spending—remain in the hands of the central government. This was the case with the so-called CODER (Regional Economic Development Councils) which consisted of regional representatives and civil servants whose function was primarily consultative in forming the economic plan. Similarly, a degree of decentralization was attained when the departmental councils were given some, although very limited, jurisdiction over spending without prior approval of the central organs.

But neither the department nor the region was given genuine freedom to tax and to spend the monies they raised to develop its own administrative practices or its educational institutions with an eye to local needs. No department or region was given the right to proceed with what is called the "police powers" of the states in the United States —or even the American cities—covering a variety of things such as hospitals, schools, zoning, land use, educational policies, highways, and so on. Even municipal roads could not be decided upon without approval from the top. The only exception was perhaps garbage collection, but this too came under detailed regulation from the central authorities.

Decentralization was to many only a palliative. What was needed they claimed was genuine autonomy; the heart of such an autonomy consisted of the power to tax and to spend in order to give to regions the "police powers." In 1970 the CODER committees were abolished in favor of regional assemblies, of which half were deputies and mayors and half were elected representatives from the regions. But they did not supersede the indestructible *préfet* and their functions were limited to consultations concerning the economic plan.

What in effect the advocates of "genuine" regionalism demand is the freedom of the citizens and the associational groups to make decisions that are binding upon all within the region and cannot be vetoed or nullified by the central state. Large urban centers that have or will soon have one million inhabitants—Lyon, Marseille, Nice, Lille, Strasbourg—demand similar autonomous powers. It is one way to release grassroots initiative and also to unburden centralized administrative machinery that is increasingly unable to supervise the activities of the whole country. Such regionalism will lead to what might be called a "qualified pluralism": the central government confines its activities to essentially national issues—defense, foreign affairs, social legislation, budgetary appropriations, taxation, economic planning—and the regional and urban centers receive independent powers for a specified set of activities and concurrent powers for others. In the latter case, consultation between the central organ and the regional organs will be the rule.

There is every reason to expect that reforms in this direction are likely. First, many Gaullists (despite the strong Jacobinist element in the party), and the Left have advocated drastic reform toward regional autonomy. Together they represented more than 70 percent of the votes on the first ballot of the presidential election. Second, the central administration, despite its vested interests to delay and obstruct such reform, is beginning to suffer under the burdens of its total administrative responsibilities. It simply cannot do what it was expected to do when the state was a limited one, when agriculture was the important economic activity, and when more than 60 percent of the French lived in hamlets, villages and small towns. With almost 30 percent of the economic activity in the hands of the State, directly or indirectly; with the growth of metropolitan centers; with the enormous growth of provincial universities and with the need to adapt economic planning to a highly selective and differentiated set of choices and priorities (as opposed to the relatively simple task of industrializing, as was the case in the earlier years) decentralization or regionalism emerge as more economic and rational administrative patterns. Professor Crozier is right in saying that the present system is anachronistic and irrational. It is in the process of changing.

Educational Reform

Rapid industrialization inevitably made its impact felt upon the educational structures. Geared to the nineteenth century bourgeois society, it catered to a small elite. The heart of the system was the secondary educational system—the lycée—emphasizing the traditional disciplines with a stiff terminal examination that applied uniformly throughout France. The best students found their way to highly specialized schools training for law, teaching, medicine, the civil service, the Ministry of Finance, and the other top state organs. The system provided for continuing elites rather than renovating them. Most of the children remained outside. The system perpetuated social stratification and impeded communication among different groups in the French society. Crozier refers to it as a "caste system."

With no more than 100,000 or so lycées graduates and no more than a total 75,000 university students until World War II, the system, despite its social injustices, seemed adequate. It was kept and defended thanks to the infiltration—indeed the colonization—of the Ministry of Education, by powerful elite groups among the lycée teachers and university professors. These groups wanted to continue to perpetuate their own position in the educational world. But this system can no longer survive.

The logic of industrialization runs counter to a closed educational system. First, it calls for the development (and hence the training) of specialized and highly differentiated skills. The need for technical education providing openings for the white collar and managerial positions becomes a necessity; second, it encourages the recruitment of elites on the basis of achievement rather than status; third, by creating a consumer ethic it has an egalitarian impact upon expectations and attitudes of those in underprivileged "castes." Finally, the very differentiation of tasks in the administration itself, in charge of economic activities and planning and the application of technology can hardly be accommodated with recruitment through the traditional educational techniques—in law, politics, and public administration.

The need for differentiated skills, the demand for technical training and recruitment on the basis of talent could not be undertaken without a vast reform in the educational structures and practices. The Gaullist system created the quantitative conditions for change—the building of new universities, the enormous growth in the student body and the development of technical education. In June 1974 there were more students taking their annual secondary degree examination (325,000 in all) than there were students in all the lycées in France in 1939. Even so, the overall emphasis had been on uniformity; on large classroom instruction; on individual mastery of abstract topics rather than cooperative learning through experimentation and concrete application to problem-solving.

The university remained large and anonymous and its impersonality became even more obvious as the student body grew in numbers. The demand for individual attention; for innovation; for new methods of learning; for changes in the curriculum to meet both the new needs of students and the needs of the society became irresistible. So was the students' demand to be treated as full participants in the educational decisions rather than as passive recipients of instruction imparted by their elders. The events of May–June 1968, when the students went to the streets, occupied the universities, manhandled a number of the professors and even some of the Ministers had an objective reason.[7] The student uprising was based upon a genuine desire to reform the university both in the instruction it provided and in the highly centralized method through which the Minister of Education controlled the substance of education. It led to the great reform of 1968, which was to many only a beginning. It provided for a greater degree of autonomy for each university to devise its curriculum and methods of instruction; some financial autonomy; and full participation of students to vote for the selection of the top administrators.

The years between 1969 and 1973, however, were again years of hesitation if not retrenchment. Sporadic outbreaks of violence in the universities spread increasingly among the secondary school students. The Minister of Education and the privileged groups among professors began to reassert their control and return to past practices. The students became somewhat apathetic. We are entering a new cycle in which genuine reform will have to be legitimized in the name of regionalism. This can happen by allowing different university centers to develop different curricula with different methods of instruction; to permit increased specialization in subject matters that relate to student interest and societal needs and, within broader limits, to give genuine financial freedom to university authorities. Also widely recognized is the need to provide advanced training to the children of workers and farmers, to alter decisively the general examinations given for a secondary degree, to provide for adult education (or, as the French call it, "continuing education"). The need of permitting under certain conditions students who failed to enter a lycée to reapply is also conceded by all. Finally, and the point is made repeatedly by Crozier, the style of education as a whole from the first grades on tends to squelch initiative and individual curiosity. It emphasizes passive learning and unintelligent assimilation of the subject matter. The young French boys and girls learn both how to obey and to despise the rules at the earliest stages of their lives by learning what they are expected and becoming indifferent to what they have learned. Nonparticipation is inculcated at the school.

Every society develops its own norms of assimilating the young into its own values and practices. Few societies can change them overnight. The French society is no exception to this rule. But the French have not been any slower than the British or the Germans to modify encrusted and old-fashioned practices. On the contrary, despite the many critics, the French have not only become conscious of the need for change but are in the process of undertaking a rapid transformation in their educational system, more so than many other European countries. The very size of the student body; the efforts to provide greater student participation; the development of provincial universities; the beginnings of decentralization both of the universities and within the university; the addition of new subject matters and new teaching and research units corresponding to the "Departments" of American universities, all constitute evidence of ferment and change. It is very unlikely that the system will approximate that of the Americans—highly pluralistic and perhaps chaotic. It is far more likely that as with regionalization, a balance will be struck between the prerequisites of uniformity and centralization, on the one hand, and pluralism and differentiation on the other. The French university is about to become the servant of the nation and its people rather than of a privileged class.

Attaining Participation

One means of promoting participation is, as we mentioned above, regionalism. Another means—often referred to by the French as "concer-

tation" (that is, acting in concert; acting together)—calls for a direct interplay and cooperation not only at local and regional levels but also at the national level, between those who make decisions and those who are affected. It applies to economic decisions such as planning, social welfare, wages, pensions; to university and educational policies as they affect the students and teachers; to the nationalized sector of the economy as it affects the consumers. In most cases *concertation* involves a tripartite form of consultation that includes the two parties involved and the State acting not only through the civil service but also through Ministers and at times even the Prime Minister.

Concertation is beginning to be an accepted formula. Thus before deciding on wage policies and related economic issues affecting the workers, the Prime Minister held in June 1974, meetings with the trade union leaders and the representatives of the industry. It was in a similar meeting that drastic improvements to workers' earnings were made in 1968. The agricultural associations are directly consulted prior to decisions on the agricultural prices. Allocations for regions are decided after similar consultations through the regional assemblies. It is not a process that is as yet fully legitimized, however. The workers—especially those with Communist leadership—fear that constant dialogue with the managers and industrialists will undermine the class feeling that the trade unions want to perpetuate; the business groups prefer to pass on the responsibility to the State rather than engage in a confrontation with the unions.

But *concertation* is gaining ground. If extended and legitimized it will provide for a "face to face" relationship between various groups, even if under the auspices of the State. It will, in other words, undermine considerably Crozier's contention that groups and individuals shy away from cooperative problem-solving and prefer to pass on to the State responsibilities that they are unwilling to assume. The system will become more cooperative and more participatory and with it the joint responsibility for decisions made will bind the citizens closer together instead of separating them from each other and from the State.

Reforming the Industrial Firm

A particular type of *concertation* relates to the firm—the central decision-making industrial unit in a modern society. Depending on its size, the firm includes the top manager, the managerial personnel, the clerical personnel, the white collar workers, foremen, technicians, and of course the workers. One type of "participation" is to connect the firm, whenever it is possible, with those for whom its products are destined: the specific categories of consumers or the consumer-at-large. In some cases, when the firm is large or belongs to the public sector (which is often the same), this is not difficult. When the firm is small it becomes virtually impossible.

A second type of participation envisaged is internal to the activities and decisions of the firm. There are three kinds of decisions involved: one relates to the profitability of the product and the sharing of all in the profits; another to the decisions that go beyond considerations of profitability to include overall social considerations, such as the quality of the product and the advisability of producing it; finally, there are the decisions regarding the internal workings of the firm—that is, the conditions under which its members work.

Genuine *concertation* between firm and consumer has taken the form of the traditional consumer councils. With regard to some of the firms in the public sector—in electricity, gas, and transportation, for instance—there are committees of "usagers," those who use the services. With regard to profit-sharing, it was the Gaullist design to develop it as fully as possible, thus reducing the conflict between workers and managers. It was hailed by many as "the third way"—transcending both Socialism and capitalism. This hope has not materialized but profit-sharing is expanding rapidly and so have the benefits to the workers.

As for participation in deciding on the working conditions in the factory, the law makes it mandatory for workers' committees to be elected in all factories employing more than fifty workers. Thus it can cover a sizable part of the working force if strictly applied. The committees meet with the managerial personnel and discuss all matters pertaining to the firm and they run social services subsidized by the employers.

"Industrial democracy" involving the participation of all members of a firm, all members of the same industry and conceivably all consumers, is not a new theory. It was evoked by many social writers in the nineteenth century both in France and in England. The fact that it has gained so much prominence in the thinking of contemporary French sociologists and politicians—especially among the Gaullists and left-wing Socialists as well—indicates the constant search for a formula to reduce social conflicts, to emancipate the individual and especially the workers from the anonymity and impersonality of their everyday working life to give them a personal involvement and interest in their work. The double opposition from the industrialists and from many of the workers, especially the Communist trade unions, accounts for the small gains made thus far. But a degree of "self-government" in industry is becoming more and more accepted.

Radio and Television

Radio and television have been a state monopoly. They are administered through the O.R.T.F. (Radio and Television Office of France), and rigorously controlled by the government, which has used them as a means of propaganda excluding opposing views and presenting government policies and officials in a favorable light. The government has constantly intervened in the decisions made by the Directors. Many of them were arbitrarily removed to be replaced by new ones. The opposition and broad segments of the public have been sharply critical. Almost everybody is in favor of keeping the O.R.T.F. as a state monopoly rather than turning it over or even turning over some stations and one channel to private hands. Many would prefer to see a public and genuinely autonomous corporation—something like the British Broadcasting Corporation in Britain—established.

But the problem does not lie only in the present organization of the office but also in the content of its programs and even more in how decisions on what to produce and disseminate are made. There is a tendency to propagate one point of view, one type of culture and make it the channel for some to the exclusion of others. Similarly, it is argued that there is not enough genuine decentralization to allow for regional and local stations to develop topics of local current or cultural interest. Thus there is the double demand for broader participation at the national level to provide for differentiated programs and for greater local and regional autonomy.

The reorganization of radio and television actually under consideration is one of the most sensitive issues and the answer to be given will be a crucial indication of the direction in which the new government plans to move. It is linked to the demand for genuine freedom of expression not only political but also cultural and religious. It is above all part and parcel of the demand to put an end to statism and turn over the national media to the cultural, political, religious, and voluntary groups and associations, enabling them to express fully their views. It defies one of the strongest traditions in France, just as strong as that of a highly centralized State: the unity of its culture and the role of the State in maintaining and propagating it.

The Prospects for Reform

All the above reforms—in education, in the administration of the State, in radio and television, in the firm—constitute what the French call "structural reforms." The socialization of some nine key industrial activities advocated by the Left related to structural reforms in the economy. But some leftist groups favor industrial democracy and self-government in the firm rather than socialization for fear that the latter would add to the existing bureaucratization and centralization of the French system and thus increase the dominant role of the State.

What are the prospects for the new government and the new President of the Republic? Giscard d'Estaing promised change and reform but "without risks." He put his faith in continuing industrial growth. But he made promises that call for immediate incremental changes and also for some major, perhaps structural, changes of the administration and the society.

With regard to the economy the new President has been moving to smooth out the rough edges of inequality. The minimum wage was raised to about $1.45 an hour; working hours were limited to 43 hours a week; special provisions have been made to avoid arbitrary lay-offs of workers; special arrangements are in progress to provide for a period of retraining and to subsidize the young people who are looking for jobs. Also, sweeping measures were announced to provide a guaranteed wage for one year in case of unemployment. Yet, no serious effort has been made to modify the tax system, another area that is crying for reform. Only some minor modifications have been introduced to help the low salaried groups and to tax more highly the corporation and the high income brackets. Indirect taxes continue to remain heavy. Those on old-age pensions received additional benefits but they have corresponded thus far to the rise in the cost of living.

The dilemma facing the new government is how to maintain industrial growth without inflation. To slow down growth through drastic fiscal policies and control of credit would be to create unemployment, which would be far more disastrous than maintaining the existing inequalities. To reduce sharply the inequalities, on the other hand, requires additional expenditures that would only add to the inflationary spiral. Caught between the two, the government may be unable to change drastically and quickly the economic conditions of everyday life for any and all.

The prospects for reform, however, in the other areas we discussed are not subject to the constraints that apply to the economy. Many of the critics of the new President point out that he and his government are backed by the conservative forces in the country and that though lip service was paid to reform he has neither the will nor the support to go ahead with it. This is true as far as the electoral support for the President in the presidential election goes. But electoral support and public support are not the same. The new President is aware that a reformist policy is the only one that is likely to gain him the support of many of the Gaullists and of the Left. He has the time to fashion ad hoc majorities in the National Assembly that can enact reforms while strengthening his public support and cutting into the strength of the Gaullists and the Left. The new legislative election is scheduled for 1978 and the presidential one for 1981. If this is not to become known as the decade of reform, it will become one of serious social conflict that will undermine the stability of the Gaullist institutions, and indeed may bring the Gaullist legacy to an end.

Concluding Note

One of the best indicators of the effectiveness of a political system is its ability to translate conflict into legitimate decisions and to provide the governmental instrumentalities that can do it. The French polity ever since 1958 has had its ample share of conflict, sporadic outbreaks of protest and violent demonstrations and, as we noted, witnessed the outbreak of what amounted to a virtual revolution in May–June 1968. But the system held; what is more it seems to have gained progressively the acceptance of the vast majority of the French. The ease with which the presidential succession was carried out both after DeGaulle's resignation in 1969, and even more, in 1974 when only a small margin of votes separated the two candidates indicates not only its viability but its vitality. The Gaullist system, as we outlined in the first chapter, seems to be functioning well at a time when countries with a solid democratic tradition of stability, like Britain, seem to be unable to manage conflict and provide the basis of compromise from which acceptable policies may emerge. It is functioning well at a time when most other Western parliamentary democracies face continuing crises.

I have tried to show in this book that the present stability and related effectiveness of the French government is the result of two major forces: one is institutional, embodied in the Gaullist constitutional design of presidential government; the second lies in the socioeconomic changes of the French society that I have outlined with reference to its economic and social modernization.

The two reinforce each other. Institutional changes have provided for political leadership that stems directly from the people through a presidency that speaks for the whole nation and can act decisively in times of crisis. This is the "unifying" element in the Gaullist legacy. Socioeconomic changes, on the other hand, have accounted for the gradual breakdown of class antagonisms, of regional and ideological disparities and conflict, and the development of great interest and involvement of the French in their political system—that is, participation. This in turn has led to the breakdown of the old political parties that reflected the traditional particularisms and cleavages and the emergence of national parties—even if they are coalition parties—that attempt to synthesize diverse points of view in the form of political platforms designed to attract the voters in support of one government or another. The changing nature of the Communist party has helped to form a left-wing coalition that has governmental vocation and has shed sectarian and revolutionary approaches. The cooperation of the centrists with the Gaullists, on the other hand, has produced a broad centrist, but enlightened and reformist, coalition. Giscard d'Estaing is the beneficiary of the latter and his ability to govern and maintain the system will be measured more by his ability to reform than to maintain the support of those who voted for him. The centrist majority is behind him, but the presidency cannot ignore the Gaullist legacy for movement and reform shared not only by many orthodox Gaullists but also by the Left. His chances of appealing to both, of cutting across classes and Left-Right divisions, through reforms that, as we have seen, have been gathering momentum throughout the years of Pompidou's presidency will not only revive the Gaullist tradition but will ensure the ongoing effectiveness of the political system that DeGaulle and his associates launched fifteen years ago. Not only the Gaullist legacy but also the Gaullist dream of national unity and rapid social reform remain intact.

ENDNOTES

1. In *Revue de la Défense Nationale,* July, 1974 (Paris).

2. The best account of the problem is undoubtedly in Stanley Hoffmann's last chapter "The State: For What Society" in his *Decline or Renewal, France since the 1930's,* pp. 443–86.

3. Ibid., pp. 146–47 and p. 495.

4. Philip Williams and Martin Harrison, *Politics and Society in DeGaulle's Republic,* p. 280.

5. *Le Monde,* June 25, 1974, p. 22.

6. Charles DeGaulle, *Discours et Messages,* Vol. 5, (Paris: Plon, 1972), pp. 385–86.

7. Bernard E. Brown, *The French Revolt: May 1968* (New York: The McCaleb-Seiles Publishing Co., 1970).

General Bibliography

CHAPTER ONE: The Gaullist Legacy

1. Roy Macridis and Bernard Brown, *The DeGaulle Republic: Quest for Unity* (Homewood, Ill.: The Dorsey Press, 1961).

2. Jean Lacouture, *DeGaulle,* trans. Francis K. Price (London: Hutchinson, 1970).

3. Charles DeGaulle, *The War Memoirs of Charles DeGaulle,* 3 volumes, trans. Richard Howard (New York: Simon and Schuster, 1960).

4. Charles DeGaulle, *Memoirs of Hope, Renewal and Endeavor,* trans. Terence Kilmartin (New York: Simon and Schuster, 1971).

5. Robert Aron, *An Explanation of DeGaulle,* trans. Marianne Sinclair (New York: Harper and Row, 1966).

6. Philip Williams and Martin Harrison, *Politics and Society in DeGaulle's Republic* (New York: Doubleday; Anchor, 1973).

7. Philip Williams, *The French Parliament: Politics in the Fifth Republic* (New York: Frederick A. Praeger, 1968).

8. Stanley Hoffman, *Decline or Renewal: France since the 1930's* (New York: Viking Press, 1974).

9. Roy Macridis, *DeGaulle: Implacable Ally* (New York: Harper and Row, 1966).

10. Jean Charlot, *Le Phenomène Gaulliste* (Paris: Fayard, 1970).

11. Jean Charlot, *Les Français et DeGaulle* (Paris: Plon, 1971).

12. Maurice Parodi, *L'Economie et la Société Française de 1945 à 1970* (Paris: Armand Colin, 1971).

CHAPTER TWO: The Pompidou Years (1969–1973): Gaullism Without DeGaulle

1. Maurice Duverger, *La Monarchie Républicaine* (Paris: Robert Laffont, 1974).

2. Giles Martinet, *Le Système Pompidou* (Paris: Seuil, 1973).

3. Charles Debbasch, *La France de Pompidou* (Paris: Presses Universitaires de France, 1974).

CHAPTER THREE: The Evolution of the Political Forces and the Legislative Election of 1973

1. Pierre Avril, *Politics in France* (London: Pelican, 1969).

2. Philip Williams, with David Goldey and Martin Harrison, *French Politicians and Elections 1951–1969* (London: Cambridge University Press, 1970).

3. Henry Erhmann, *Politics in France,* 3d ed. (Boston: Little, Brown, 1974).

4. Roy Macridis and Robert Ward, *Modern Political Systems, Europe*, 3d ed. (Englewood Cliffs, N.J.: Prentice-Hall, 1972), pp. 149–307.

5. Beer and Ulam, *Patterns of Government,* 3d ed., (New York: Random House, 1973), pp. 333–470.

6. Roy Macridis, *The Modernization of French Politics: The Legislative Election of March 1973,* University Programs Modular Studies, General Learning Press, 1974.

CHAPTER FOUR: The Presidential Election of May 1974

The only available documentary survey with interpretative articles is: *L'Election Présidentielle de Mai 1974* in *Le Monde* (Dossiers et Documents), May 1974, Paris. Also, A. Lancelot, "Elections: la relève et le sursis," in *Projet,* September–October, 1974, pp. 941–58.

CHAPTER FIVE: Beyond Gaullism: What Kind of State for What Kind of Society

1. Stanley Hoffmann, *Decline or Renewal: France since the 1930's,* pp. 443–486.

2. Michel Crozier, *The Stalled Society* (New York: Viking Press, 1973).

3. Jean-Claude Colliard, *Les Républicains Indépendants: Valéry Giscard d'Estaing* (Paris: Presses Universitaires de France, 1972).

4. André Pautard, *Valéry Giscard d'Estaing,* (Paris: Edipa, 1974).